CONTENTS

Warman's®
U.S. Stamps
FIELD GUIDE 2nd Edition

JOHN WAYNE
37 USA
2004

10 U.S. POSTAGE 10

U.S. POSTAGE
24 CENTS 24

4¢
u.s.
Christmas 1962

Maurice D. Wozniak

Published by

Krause Publications, a division of F+W Media, Inc.
700 East State Street • Iola, WI 54990-0001
715-445-2214 • 888-457-2873
www.krausebooks.com

To order books or other products call toll-free 1-800-258-0929
or visit us online at www.krausebooks.com or www.Shop.Collect.com

ISBN-13: 978-1-4402-1699-2
ISBN-10: 1-4402-1699-1

*Special thanks to Mystic Stamp Co. for providing
some of the stamp images that made this book possible.*
800-433-7811 • www.mysticstamp.com

Designed by Donna Mummery
Edited by Dan Brownell

Printed in China

INTRODUCTION

THE WORLD'S OLDEST HOBBY

Stamp collecting is generally accepted as the world's oldest hobby, dating to the introduction of prepaid adhesive stamps to indicate the payment of mailing fees in Great Britain in 1840. The Universal Postal Union, an international postal watchdog and clearinghouse, estimates that 30 million people around the world collect stamps today, and retail sales in the hobby total $10 billion annually.

It is safe to say no two collections are alike. An entire library of books on the hobby would be needed to cover all its nuances. This handy field guide is only a brief and basic introduction to one area of philately—the collecting of United States stamps, which is the most popular specialization in America.

We hope the information you'll find here will whet your appetite to pursue this hobby enthusiastically and find the enjoyment that so many generations of stamp collectors who preceded you have already found.

STATE OF THE MARKET

In general, the stamp collecting market has been stable for many years.

It is a changing market that is reaching maturity in the United States, in terms of the age of its participants and their sophistication. Local stamp clubs are populated with gray-haired members, men and women, and surveys of subscribers to the dwindling numbers of national publications that cover the hobby indicate that their average age is in the mid-60s. There are fewer stamp stores, fewer stamp clubs, probably fewer stamp collectors than there were 50 years ago.

But attendance at large stamp shows remains robust. At international and national shows, more than 100 dealers may participate, and hundreds of collectors' exhibits, featuring displays that show scholarly studies of a single issue through wide-ranging examinations of more elaborate themes, will be on view.

The market demographics have changed. In the mid-20th century the U.S. Post Office Department estimated there were several million stamp collectors and catered to them. Children and teenagers, who had considerably less mobility and leisure options than today, were encouraged to collect stamps. Many Americans were convinced that they could buy stamps and sell them years later for a profit. So many of them were not collectors at all but would-be investors.

That frustrated expectation of profit from the hobby has colored people's perception of the stamp market today.

Aside from a speculative bubble that burst in the early 1980s, the market (measured in dollars) has plodded steadily, but not spectacularly, upward.

The growth of Internet marketing by professional dealers and collectors alike has spurred the hobby. Further, stamp collecting has branched into popular areas such as topicals and postal history, which has added dimension and enthusiasm to the hobby and will help propel it into the future.

WHY COLLECT?

Everyone has his or her own reason to collect stamps, and some reasons may be completely unique to individual collectors. But most collectors will admit to a few common interests:

Fun: This has to be the underlying factor of any hobby; without the element of enjoyment any activity would be a job or a task. But if you enjoy looking for a stamp to add to your collection, appreciate the significance of a stamp or an envelope, or thrill to an unexpected discovery, the effort becomes a pleasant pastime. With each addition to your collection your horizon expands, and your vision of what you'd like it to become expands as well.

History: The subjects on U.S. stamps represent famous people, places and events of the nation's past or, in many issues of recent years, popular culture. Call it nostalgia, appreciation or education; history plays a major role in many collections.

Technology: From the fine engraving of early intaglio stamps to the full-color gravure of today, the printer's art is on display in stamps. From tiny "secret marks" used to distinguish some early stamps to almost microscopic nicks and spots to "hidden images" that can be seen only with special lenses, stamps carry an array of attractions for the technophile.

Art: Some stamp subjects, such as scenes from our national parks, are original art, created especially for the medium of the postage stamp. Others are exquisitely detailed, tiny reproductions of larger originals. Artists themselves have been commemorated on stamps. A collector could concentrate entirely on this aspect, but visually every stamp collection is essentially an artistic display of its owner's creation.

Relaxation: Stamp collecting, with its demand for careful attention, provides an escape from the cares of the day. This immersion is different from fun, which is a more overt appreciation. Heads of state have used their stamp collections as refuge during times of war, and captains of industry as well as common people escape to stamps to clear their minds from daily strife.

Investment: Yes, you can make a profit in stamp collecting, as with many other hobbies. For some, the profit motive is their main interest. But most stamp collectors see their hobby as a diversion and lack the kind of discipline and concentration needed to buy low and sell high in every transaction. With that said, it is arguably better to acquire the best-looking stamps you can find to fill the gaps in your collection, from standpoints of aesthetics and value. Also, understand that classic and scarce stamps tend to rise in value, while common, inexpensive stamps remain common and cheap.

WHAT TO COLLECT?

The traditional way to collect stamps is to acquire an album that has spaces for all of a country's stamps, along with their pictures, and mount the stamps as you acquire them in the spaces provided. Many people branch out from there. They might specialize in one series or even a single stamp with many varieties. They might collect covers, envelopes or wrappers bearing the stamps they like. Maybe they'll collect stamps depicting sports, animals or flowers if those topics dovetail with their other interests.

Some people collect only postally-used stamps. Others seek the finest-looking unused stamps they can find. If you decide to collect postmarks or covers you'll probably want to create your own storage system or album.

You may want to combine collectibles. Autographs of the artists or the stamp subjects can be challenging, for example. Picture postcards, especially those that have gone through the mail, can add color and interest. Sports cards and stamps fit nicely together. One nice thing about a hobby with so many facets is that you can collect whatever pleases you.

HOW TO COLLECT

Stamp collecting, as a solitary hobby, can be immensely satisfying. But sharing the experience with others adds another dimension. As a beginner, you may find guidance and appreciation among members of a stamp club. As a more experienced collector, you will find satisfaction in sharing your knowledge with others, whether by helping a beginner past pitfalls or profiting from the advice of an expert. Learning together is mutually beneficial.

Most regional stamp clubs meet monthly and welcome beginners. A good club will have a program of interest to the members, a business session at which projects and social activities will be discussed, and time for members to "show and tell." Many clubs allot time before or after meetings for members to trade or buy and sell stamps among themselves.

Other clubs exist for collectors with similar specific interests, such as pre-canceled stamps or postal history. They might publish a regular bulletin listing information and activities and may meet only once a year at a stamp show. An Internet search may turn up clubs that interest you. One of the national periodicals for stamp collectors may be a big help. Also, philatic organizations are listed in the Resources section of this book.

HOW TO FIND STAMPS

If you decide to collect only stamps that come to you in your mail or to your company's mailroom, your options will be extremely limited and growing smaller. Even your local post office probably will not carry each stamp issued by the U.S Postal Service. But the hobby of stamp collecting is well organized and dynamic, and you have many sources of stamps.

Tell the people who write to you that you collect stamps, and ask them to use commemorative stamps on their letters. Ask relatives, neighbors and friends to save for you the envelopes they receive. Ask acquaintances if they have old mail or even old stamp collections they will share with you. Most of the people you ask will tell you "no," but once in a while you may be lucky.

Check the wastebasket in the post office lobby. Many people who rent boxes sort through their mail on-site and simply throw away envelopes either after opening them or without opening them. You can find interesting uses of stamps and postmarks, even on so-called "junk mail." You can search other trash baskets and containers of clean waste also—if you aren't unduly embarrassed.

You can buy newly issued stamps, even those with limited distribution, by mail from the USPS. Collectors who have been in the hobby for many years tend to accumulate a lot of duplicate stamps. They would love to see those duplicates go to a good new home.

Many stamp dealers advertise free or low-priced stamps to attract customers. You will find their ads in philatelic publications, and you will find dealers at stamp shows, which are held in most urban areas from time to time. There are relatively few stamp stores but a lot of retail dealers who sell to collectors via mail order or the Internet.

If you buy packets of stamps from dealers, be aware that the supposed value of those stamps probably is inflated. Catalog publishers assign a base price of 20c to even the most commonly used stamp, and dealers will cite that supposed value when marketing their packets. Thus, 100 of the most commonly used U.S. stamps might have a so-called "catalog value" of $20, even though you might find the same stamps in a dealer's bulk box for a fraction of that amount. The same warning applies to collections you might find occasionally at estate sales and antique stores.

At stamp clubs you will find collectors who will be willing to help you get started in the hobby—with advice, if not with stamps. If you can't find a stamp club where you live, try starting one yourself. You can start with just two people who get together every month or so to have a good time talking about your hobby and agree to actively search for other collectors.

You may be able to trade duplicate stamps with collectors in other parts of the country. Look for their classified ads for trades in stamp publications.

Once you have an understanding of the market you might want to try your hand at stamp auctions, which take bids in person, by mail, by telephone, and via the Internet.

WHAT SHOULD STAMPS COST?

Rarity doesn't count for everything in fixing the price of stamps, but it is a factor.

Popularity is another factor. So is eagerness to buy— and desperation to sell. It works both ways.

You can get some idea of the current market by looking at some stamps of 1993. In that year, the big news, driven by a months-long campaign, swirled around a stamp for Elvis Presley, the deceased "King of Rock 'n' Roll." Stamp collectors were not the only ones who bought that stamp when it came out. So did music fans, speculators, and people who figured they could use the stamp to make displays they could sell to music fans. Many millions of "Elvis" and "Elvis Presley" stamps were sold to people who had no intention of using them on a letter.

Also in 1993, with considerably less promotion, the postal service issued a stamp for Hank Williams, another deceased music icon.

Today, you can find unused Presley and Williams stamps in dealers' face-value lots. They retail about $1—except for a perforation variety of a Hank Williams sheet stamp that has a catalog value of $25 unused and $10 used.

Although many collectors of U.S. stamps want their

examples to look like they just came out of a post office drawer, some collectors prefer canceled stamps. Most used stamps, except those issued up until 1930 or so, can be obtained for pennies—literally. Even if you decide to collect unused stamps, those that are still valid for postage, you'll be able to find most of them issued since the 1930s at face value—or even less—in dealers' stocks.

You'll find attractive used U.S. stamps that are 125 to 150 years old for less than $10 in dealers' stocks. At the other end of the scale, some U.S. stamps, used or unused, sell for thousands—even hundreds of thousands—of dollars each.

If, like most stamp collectors, you do not have an unlimited budget, you should remain realistic: Collect the best-quality stamps that appeal to you and you can afford. As you learn more about the hobby you may be able to pick up some bargains in stamp varieties that go unrecognized by others.

The chances are slim that you may one day stumble across a fabulously valuable stamp, but such an event has occurred before and probably will again. In fact, collectors today are finding production-error stamps more frequently than ever before.

HANDLING AND COLLECTING

Treat your stamp collection with respect. Remember that it consists of little pieces of paper that are already contaminated with ink and adhesive as well as oils from people's fingers and tongues.

The main thing you need to be a proper collector is a good attitude. Your goal is to examine and enjoy stamps without damaging them further. Certainly, keep them away from fire and flood. Additionally, protect them from spilled liquids and light and the acids that are in most papers.

Learn to use stamp tongs, specialized tweezers whose smooth ends can hold even a wet stamp firmly without damaging it. Don't use your fingers, which have natural oils and other dirt.

Use a commercial or homemade album, stock sheets with acid-free paper, or inert plastic to store and display your stamps. Hinge them gently or carefully insert them into all-over plastic mounts to hold them in place. Removing hinges can damage stamps. Get advice from experienced collectors, and always remember damage cannot be undone.

HOW TO JUDGE QUALITY

If you have a choice between two copies of a particular stamp to add to your collection—one dirty, torn, and crushed and the other bright and pristine—you probably would choose the latter. You know, without any formal training, what you find attractive, and in general that inherent eye will serve you well as you try to determine the differences in quality.

With a practiced eye, you can learn quickly how to judge or grade the quality of a stamp. You must scrutinize the front and the back of the stamp and compare it to standards you have learned and other stamps you have seen.

First, is it used or unused? A used stamp might have only a barely discernible cancellation mark—or even none at all—and might even retain most of its adhesive. Cancellations should be light and leave the main design elements of the stamp exposed.

An unused stamp whose gum has been disturbed, even in the most minor way, such as a hint of a hinge removal, will not qualify as a mint-quality stamp. If it has never gone through the mail, but its gum has been soaked off, its value may be greatly diminished.

If the perforations (or scissor separations on early

stamps) cut into the design on just one side it is considered to have "average" centering. On a "fine" stamp, the central design will be away from the perforations all around. "Very Fine" stamps approach centering perfection, and "Extra Fine" or "Superb" stamps are indeed perfect.

Bright-colored ink with no scrapes or scratches on the front is most desirable. Chemicals or light must not alter color.

Original gum with no marks (as noted above) is preferable to a stamp that has been re-gummed. Adding adhesive to a stamp that has none is a fraud; its only purpose is to cover up some fault and cheat a buyer.

The best-quality stamps will have no faults. The perforation teeth all around will be the same length. The paper will have no thin spots—from careless removal of a hinge, for example. The stamp must not be torn or even creased. It must not be stained from a liquid spill or mildew, for example. Especially with modern stamps, the cancellation must not be done with ink pen or marker. Even though it once was not uncommon to display stamps for sale by pinning them to a board, today those pinholes are considered damage.

BOGUS STAMPS

While fake and forged stamps exist, sometimes in significant numbers, they generally do not pose a threat to the wary philatelist, for two reasons. First, most United States stamps are relatively inexpensive and thus provide little incentive to the manufacturing of bogus items. Second, for those stamps that are sufficiently valuable to attract the criminal element, respected authentication services exist to help collectors sort the real from the false.

It is instructive to differentiate stamp fakery by its intent: Is it a counterfeit intended to defraud the postal service, or is it a fake intended to fool a collector? We might add a third category, the practical joke, by which a stamp image is manipulated to create a wonderment.

Some counterfeits of classic engraved stamps are so expertly done that they bring prices on the collecting market that rival the stamps they imitate. Many others are so crudely executed that they fail a close examination.

In recent years, however, the proliferation of high-resolution color copiers and printing equipment have made the illegal reproduction of stamps more difficult to detect.

For the collector, the most insidious fakes are those created by dishonest individuals to make one stamp look like another (more valuable) one or to disguise faults that would affect a stamp's price. Perforations may be added or trimmed away, adhesive may be restored, or overprints may be added, for example.

Commercial "expertizers" can provide certification of a stamp's identity. Contact information of some can be found in the Resources section of this book.

WHERE ARE ALL THE STAMPS?

Almost every stamp issued by the United States in the last century and a half is still valid for postage. Of course, most of the early ones exist only in collections or in dealers' stocks. Still, it's not unheard of to find a 75-year-old stamp used today on a letter from a stamp collector.

The search for stamps is a treasure hunt that drives the hobby. If you let others know of your hobby you may gain access to an old collection that's no longer being used, or a stash of old stamps that someone's relative kept in a drawer, or a packet of old letters saved in an attic.

COLLECTING THE WORLD

Collecting the stamps of the world, unless you impose strict limits on yourself, will become a never-ending task, demanding many volumes of albums and many feet of shelf space. Besides the hundreds of thousands of stamps already issued in the last century and a half, thousands more are issued every year, and even full-time dealers are hard-pressed to supply their customers. Nonetheless, many stamp collectors enjoy the pursuit of stamps of the world at some level. You can too. For example, a topical collection of birds (or any other topic) will be greatly expanded if you open it to stamps of all nations.

Another way to add a limited number of foreign stamps to your U.S. collection is to include the foreign counterparts to joint-issue stamps. Typically, these are commemorative stamps sharing the same basic design but issued by two countries. A third possibility would be to include American subjects featured on the stamps of other nations. A few U.S. stamps have featured foreign people, such as William Shakespeare and Winston Churchill. Likewise, some American presidents and others have appeared on foreign stamps.

INTRODUCTION TO THE LISTINGS

This field guide is not intended to be a complete catalog of every United States stamp generally regarded as being distinct. Rather, it could be considered a detailed orientation to the hobby of collecting U.S. stamps. By using this field guide, you may gain a greater knowledge and appreciation of the hobby than those who don't have a field guide. As with catalogs, values given should be considered indications, as individual prices of stamps vary considerably because of condition, availability and eagerness of the buyer and seller. Also, most specific variations in individual stamp designs are not discussed in this guide.

1847-1893

THE DAWN OF U.S. STAMPS

The first government postage stamps in the United States were authorized to take effect July 1, 1847. In Great Britain, where stamps originated seven years earlier, the first issues featured a portrait of the long-sitting Queen Victoria. But in America, Congress decided to bypass the president, James K. Polk, in favor of two giants of the nation's founding, President George Washington, whose image graced the 10-cent stamp (designated by a Roman "X"), and statesman Benjamin Franklin, who also happened to be the United States' first postmaster, on the 5-cent stamp. The two stamps were reprinted in 1875, with some differences in the images.

The 1-cent blue Franklin stamps that first appeared in 1851 tend to be distinguished by collectors according to the completeness of the ornamentation that frames the portrait. The different types appeared side-by-side on the same printing plates. Today, multiples may still be found incorporating different stamps. An unused 1-cent blue stamp with complete curlicues, known as "Type I," may have a market value of more than $200,000 today, while a similar-quality stamp with some ornamentation missing may bring less than $1,000—or even less than $100 for a canceled example.

1847	Unused	Used
5c Franklin, red-brown	$6,000	$600
10c Washington, black	$25,000	$1,500

1851-57		
1c Franklin, blue, ornamentation complete	$175,000	$45,000
1c Franklin, blue, orn. incomplete version 1	$1,100	$190
1c Franklin, blue, orn incomplete version 2	$750	$150
3c Washington, orange-brown	$3,000	$150
3c Washington, dull red	$250	$12
5c Jefferson, red-brown	$15,500	$1,100
10c Washington, green, top orn. trimmed	$25,000	$1,600
10c Washington, green, side orn. cut	$3,000	$275
12c Washington, black	$4,000	$375

5c Franklin red-brown   *1c Franklin, blue*   *5c Jefferson, red-brown*   *12c Washington, black*

THE FIRST PERFORATED STAMPS

At first, U.S. stamps were separated for use by a scissors cut or by tearing. In 1857, the innovation of perforations was introduced on the same designs as the 1851-57 issues. Generally speaking, the imperforate versions are more valuable than the perforated versions. Therefore, collectors must be wary of a stamp with its perforations cut off and sold as an imperforate stamp.

The 5-cent Jefferson was printed in various shades of red and brown, and projections at the top and bottom of the frame design are cut away in versions known as "Type II."

More than one type may be present in multiples of the 5- and 10-cent stamps.

The 24-, 30-, and 90-cent stamps were new designs for this issue but continued the use of the same two subjects. Used examples of the high-value 90-cent stamp are valued higher than unused examples.

1857-61	Unused	Used
1c Franklin, blue, top ornamentation trimmed	$21,000	$6,250
1c Franklin, blue, side ornamentation cut	$175	$50
3c Washington, rose	$2,300	$100
3c Washington, dull red	$100	$7

1857-61	Unused	Used
5c Jefferson, brick red	$25,000	$2,300
5c Jefferson, brown	$1,200	$400
10c Washington, green, top ornamentation trimmed	$25,000	$2,500
10c Washington, green, side ornamentation cut	$275	$75
12c Washington, black	$1,400	$275
24c Washington, gray	$1,500	$375
30c Franklin, orange	$1,700	$450
90c Washington, blue	$2,700	$8,000

5c Jefferson, brick red

10c Washington, green

24c Washington, gray

30c Franklin, orange

REPRODUCTIONS AND REPRINTS

To accommodate and encourage stamp collectors, a limited number of reprints of the first two United States stamps and reproductions of the subsequent issues, sometimes in slightly different colors, were prepared by the Post Office Department in 1875. These stamps were not valid for postage. All are collectible today, and their prices generally are in the thousands of dollars. They are not listed here.

FINALLY, NEW DESIGNS

Shortly after the commencement of the American Civil War, previously-issued stamps were declared invalid. Washington, Franklin, and Thomas Jefferson continued as the only subjects of the stamp issue that began in 1861. In 1863, however, Andrew Jackson, a hero in the War of 1812 and seventh president of the U.S., took his place in the lineup. The engraved portrait encompasses nearly the entire stamp, which is known as the "Black Jack."

Then, in 1866, a stamp with the portrait of murdered President Abraham Lincoln was issued. This was significant on two counts: It was the first stamp portrait derived from a photograph—a portrait taken by C.S. German of Springfield, Ill., in 1861. And, although the Post Office Department calls it a regular-issue or ordinary stamp, its black color and timing—one year after the assassination—gave it the earmarks of a mourning or memorial issue.

The 24-cent Washington issued in shades of lilac and its color changelings are distinguishable between the two issues only by experts, and certification by an expert is desirable.

3c Washington, rose   5c Jefferson, buff   10c Washington, green

30c Franklin, orange

2c Jackson

1861-66	Unused	Used
1c Franklin, blue	$250	$45
3c Washington, pink	$8,000	$800
3c Washington, rose	$130	$3
5c Jefferson, buff	$12,000	$950
10c Washington, green	$700	$60
12c Washington, black	$1,000	$125
24c Washington, red-lilac	$2,000	$250
30c Franklin, orange	$1,500	$180

1861-66	Unused	Used
90c Washington, blue	$2,100	$450

1863-66	Unused	Used
2c Jackson	$300	$40
5c Jefferson, red-brown	$4,000	$500
5c Jefferson, brown	$1,000	$110
15c Lincoln, black	$1,500	$200
24c Washington, lilac	$1,000	$200

THE GRILL EXPERIMENT

From 1867-75, the post office experimented with patterns of tiny, embossed indentations on the then-current stamps to discourage their fraudulent re-use after cleaning to remove cancellation marks. The grill points were intended to break the fibers of the stamp paper and allow the canceling ink to be absorbed more deeply. The damaged paper made the stamps more fragile, more difficult to remove along their perforations, and more susceptible to damage when saved by collectors. The experiment ended after eight years.

Collectors differentiate grilled stamps according to the area of the grill. While some are relatively common, only a few copies are known of others, and none of these altered stamps are listed here.

1c Franklin, buff   *2c Post Horse and Rider, brown*

3c Locomotive, ultramarine   *10c Shield and Eagle, yellow*

UNAPPRECIATED CREATIVITY

In 1869, the Post Office Department launched an exuberant departure from former stamp practices, a celebration of pride in America's history and technological accomplishments—and the American people hated it. The Pictorial Series included the United States' first two-color stamps (including the first inverted-printing errors). Today collectors prize the issue, but at the time complaints poured into post offices and, within a year, the POD replaced the Pictorial Issue with more depictions of deceased statesmen.

Some stamps with these designs were specially printed in 1875 without a grill. While collectible, they are rare and are not listed here. Of the two-color stamps in this issue, all but the 90-cent Lincoln are known with frames inverted. Type II of the 15-cent issue is distinguished by a small diamond above the central illustration.

12c S.S. Adriatic, green

15c Landing of Columbus, brown and blue

24c Declaration of Independence, green and violet

30c Shield, Eagle and Flags, blue and carmine

1869	Unused	Used
1c Franklin, buff	$600	$150
2c Post Horse and Rider, brown	$400	$80
3c Locomotive, ultramarine	$250	$20
6c Washington, ultramarine	$2,000	$250
10c Shield and Eagle, yellow	$2,000	$150
12c S.S. Adriatic, green	$1,700	$150
15c Landing of Columbus, Type I	$5,000	$700
15c Landing of Columbus, Type II, brown and blue	$3,000	$275
24c Declaration of Independence, green and violet	$5,000	$750
30c Shield, Eagle and Flags, blue and carmine	$5,000	$550
90c Lincoln, carmine and black	$6,500	$2,200

1c Franklin,
ultramarine

2c Jackson, brown

3c Washington, green

6c Lincoln, red

7c Stanton
orange-vermilion

10c Jefferson, brown

BANK NOTES 1870-88

The issue represented a return to the familiar depictions of sculptural busts of presidents, statesmen and war
heroes. The name of the series derives from the printers
chosen to produce the stamps—The National Bank Note
Co., the Continental Bank Note Co., and the American Bank
Note Co. Each company, in turn, made slight changes in

*12c Henry Clay,
blackish-violet*

15c Webster, orange

*30c Hamilton,
gray-black*

*90c Perry,
rose-carmine*

2c Jackson, vermilion

5c Zachary Taylor, blue

its production of the stamps: color variations, the use of different paper, and the addition of well known "secret marks" in the ornamentation of the stamp designs. Unless a collector fully understands the nuances of this issue it is wise to seek expert certification on any of the stamps.

1870-71 with I or H grill	Unused	Used
1c Franklin, ultramarine	$1,700	$150
2c Jackson, red, brown	$925	$80
3c Washington, green	$625	$25
6c Lincoln, red	$3,500	$500
7c Edwin Stanton, vermilion	$2,800	$450
10c Jefferson, brown	$3,750	$700
12c Henry Clay, dull violet	$21,000	$3,000
15c Daniel Webster, orange	$4,500	$1,250
24c Winfield Scott, purple	---	$6,500
30c Alexander Hamilton, black	$10,500	$3,000
90c Oliver Hazard Perry, carmine	$12,000	$2,000
1870-71 without grill		
1c Franklin, ultramarine	$350	$20
2c Jackson, red, brown	$250	$12
3c Washington, green	$300	$1.25
6c Lincoln, carmine	$550	$30
7c Edwin Stanton, vermilion	$600	$90
10c Jefferson, brown	$750	$30
12c Henry Clay, dull violet	$1,500	$180
15c Daniel Webster, bright orange	$1,500	$200

1870-71 without grill	Unused	Used
24c Winfield Scott, purple	$1,300	$160
30c Alexander Hamilton, black	$5,000	$260
90c Oliver Hazard Perry, carmine	$4,000	$325
1873 CBN with secret marks		
1c Franklin, ultramarine	$195	$4.50
2c Jackson, brown	$325	$18
3c Washington, green	$110	$.65
6c Lincoln, carmine	$425	$17.50

15c Webster, red-orange

5c James Garfield

2c Washington, red-brown

4c Jackson, blue-green

4c Jackson, carmine

5c Garfield, indigo

30c Hamilton, orange-brown   *90c Perry, purple*

1873 CBN with secret marks	Unused	Used
7c Stanton, orange-vermilion	$1,110	$100
10c Jefferson, brown	$700	$25
12c Clay, blackish-violet	$1,750	$150
15c Webster, bright orange	$2,250	$200
30c Hamilton, gray-black	$2,500	$200
90c Perry, rose-carmine	$2,850	$350
1875 also by CBN		
2c Jackson, vermilion	$300	$10
5c Zachary Taylor, blue	$350	$25

1c Franklin, dull blue

2c Washington, lake

2c Washington, carmine

3c Jackson, purple

4c Lincoln, dark brown   *5c U.S. Grant, chocolate*

1879 ABN printing on soft, porous paper	Unused	Used
1c Franklin, ultramarine	$300	$4
2c Jackson, brown	$130	$3
3c Washington, green	$100	$.60
5c Taylor, blue	$550	$20
6c Lincoln, pink	$900	$30
10c Jefferson, brown, no secret mark	$1,800	$35
10c Jefferson, brown, secret mark	$1,200	$35
15c Webster, red-orange	$350	$25
30c Hamilton, full black	$1,000	$75
90c Perry, carmine	$2,000	$325

1880-81 special printing re-issue of 1869 issue by ABN, without grill, soft porous paper	Unused	Used
1c Franklin, buff	$325	$200
1c Franklin, brown-orange	$240	$175

1881-82 ABN re-engraving to some shading lines, easily detected, especially with magnification		
1c Franklin, gray-blue	$80	$1.25
3c Washington, blue-green	$80	$.75
6c Lincoln, rose	$500	$100
10c Jefferson, brown	$160	$5

1882		
5c James Garfield, yellow-brown	$275	$8

1883 ABN new denominations for reduced first-class postal rates		
2c Washington, red-brown	$45	$.50
4c Jackson, blue-green	$250	$17

1887	Unused	Used
1c Franklin, ultramarine	$80	$1.50
2c Washington, green	$40	$.30
3c Washington, vermilion	$80	$50

1888	Unused	Used
4c Jackson, carmine	$200	$20
5c Garfield, indigo	$240	$12
30c Hamilton, orange-brown	$400	$115
90c Perry, purple	$1,200	$250

1890-93 SIZES REDUCED

Designs of the stamps of the issue of 1890-93, printed by American Bank Note, were similar to the previous issue, but were smaller (approximately the size of regular-issue stamps today). Some new subjects were added to the array of famous Americans, and different shades of color were used.

A controversy over the color of the 2-cent stamp in the issue led to four varieties in the same stamp design. Originally issued in a purplish-red color known as lake, the color was changed to carmine, a more vivid red, due to complaints. (The POD called the new version "an improved quality of color.") Two constant flaws occurred in some printing plates used for the carmine versions. Tiny imperfections above the numerals in the denomination did not take up ink. The resulting oddities appear as a white bump or cap above the left numeral or both numerals.

1890-93	Unused	Used
1c Franklin, dull blue	$35	$.35
2c Washington, lake	$250	$1
2c Washington, carmine	$25	$.35

6c Garfield,
brown-red

8c William T. Sherman,
lilac

10c Webster,
green

15c Clay,
indigo

30c Jefferson, black

90c Perry, orange

1890-93	Unused	Used
2c Washington, carmine, cap on left 2	$200	$10
2c Washington carmine, cap on both 2s	$700	$20
3c Jackson, purple	$90	$6.50
4c Lincoln, dark brown	$120	$3.25
5c U.S. Grant, chocolate	$100	$3
6c Garfield, brown-red	$90	$20
8c William T. Sherman, lilac	$75	$12
10c Webster, green	$25	$3
15c Clay, indigo	$325	$25
30c Jefferson, black	$500	$35
90c Perry, orange	$800	$140

THE FIRST COMMEMORATIVES

America's first commemorative set of stamps was issued in 1893 in conjunction with the gala World's Columbian Exposition in Chicago, which celebrated the 400th anniversary of the discovery of America by Christopher Columbus.

The POD saw the celebration as a potential gold mine. It produced a large set of 16 stamps, mostly based on paintings that depicted events in the explorer's life. Five of the stamps were denominated at a dollar or more, and the relatively high

2c Landing of Columbus, "broken hat" variety

prices represented a hardship to many collectors. The annual per capita income in the U.S. was less than $250 at the time. So buying one copy of all five dollar-value stamps would represent six percent of that amount.

Interestingly, the 2-cent value in the set featured a depiction of the painting, *The Landing of Columbus* by John Vanderlyn in the U.S. Capitol in Washington, D.C. The scene was also used on the 15-cent stamp in the short-lived Series of 1869. The 2-cent Columbian in purple-maroon was

1c Columbus in Sight of Land, blue

printed in such great quantity (1,464,588,750) that it has become one of the most-saved stamps in history.

The 2-cent Columbian also has two other distinctions. First, it was the first of this set printed and therefore the first official commemorative stamp. Second, its varieties include a distinctive plate flaw that has become known as the "Broken Hat" variety. It features an easily discernible V-shaped gash in the hat of the knight standing at Columbus' left and looking down.

2c Landing of Columbus, purple-maroon

3c Flagship of
Columbus,
green

5c Columbus
Soliciting Aid of
Isabella, chocolate
brown

6c Columbus
Welcomed at
Barcelona,
purple

*8c Columbus
Restored to
Favor, magenta*

*10c Columbus
Presenting Natives,
dark brown*

*15c Columbus
Announcing His
Discovery, dark
green*

*30c Columbus
at La Rabida,
orange-brown*

*50c Recall of
Columbus,
slate blue*

*$2 Columbus in
Chains,
brown-red*

$3 Columbus Describing Third Voyage, yellow-green

$4 Isabella and Columbus, carmine

$5 Columbus, black

1893	Unused	Used
1c Columbus in Sight of Land, blue	$40	$.50
2c Landing of Columbus, purple-maroon	$40	$.25
3c Flagship of Columbus, green	$70	$28.50
4c Fleet of Columbus, blue	$115	$7.50
5c Columbus Soliciting Aid of Isabella, chocolate brown	$115	$8
6c Columbus Welcomed at Barcelona, purple	$115	$35
8c Columbus Restored to Favor, magenta	$100	$15
10c Columbus Presenting Natives, dark brown	$175	$8
15c Columbus Announcing His Discovery, dark green	$350	$85
30c Columbus at La Rabida, orange-brown	$400	$120

1893	Unused	Used
50c Recall of Columbus, slate blue	$700	$185
$1 Isabella Pledging Her Jewels, salmon	$1,650	$775
$2 Columbus in Chains, brown-red	$1,600	$750
$3 Columbus Describing Third Voyage, yellow-green	$3,250	$1,450
$4 Isabella and Columbus, carmine	$3,600	$1,700
$5 Columbus, black	$3,900	$2,050

*4c Lincoln,
dark brown*

*5c U.S. Grant,
chocolate*

*6c Garfield,
brown-red*

10c Webster, green

15c Clay, dark blue

*$1 Perry, black,
circles broken*

1894-1931

THE 'BUREAU ISSUES'

The Federal Bureau of Engraving and Printing gained its first contract for printing U.S. stamps, effective with the regular issue of 1894, and prepared almost every issue after that for more than 100 years.

The issue of 1894 is distinguished from the previous definitive set of 1890 primarily by the addition of triangle ornamentation in the upper corners of each stamp. The triangles themselves have three types: On Type I the background horizontal lines run across the triangles and are of the same thickness throughout. On Type II the horizontal lines cross the triangles but are thinner inside the inner frame line of the triangles than outside. On Type III the lines do not cross the frame lines of the triangle. The variations in triangles and in color tints make several variations of collectible stamps in the 2-cent denomination alone.

Another variation occurred in a new $1 value. On some stamps on one printing plate, the circles around the denomination are broken where they meet the curved line above (Type I); on others the circles are complete (Type II).

In 1898 the Universal Postal Union established the colors green for 1-cent stamps and blue for 5-cent stamps. Changing the colors of those stamps required changing other denominations as well to prevent confusion.

A variation similar to that of the $1 value occurred on the 10-cent value of the 1898 10-cent stamp. On Type I, the circles around the denomination do not break the oval lines above it; on Type II, the circles do break into the oval lines.

Also on that issue, the die for the 2-cent Washington stamp was redone. Besides a Type II triangle, it has other engraving differences, including a slight protrusion of the background lines of the portrait into the white oval adjacent to the "U" of "United States."

1c Franklin, ultramarine

1c Franklin, blue

2c Washington,
pink, Type I

2c Washington,
carmine-lake, Type I

2c Washington, carmine, Type I

2c Washington, carmine, Type II

*2c Washington,
carmine, Type III*

*$5 John Marshall,
dark green*

1894	Unused	Used
1c Franklin, ultramarine	$40	$5.50
1c Franklin, blue	$85	$2.25
2c Washington, pink, Type I	$35.50	$5.50
2c Washington, carmine-lake, Type I	$25	$3.50
2c Washington, carmine, Type I	$35	$1
2c Washington, carmine, Type II	$350	$10
2c Washington, carmine, Type III	$155	$10
3c Jackson, purple	$135	$10
4c Lincoln, dark brown	$200	$8.50
5c U.S. Grant, chocolate	$160	$8
6c Garfield, brown-red	$190	$27.50
8c William T. Sherman, lilac	$190	$20
10c Webster, green	$350	$12
15c Clay, dark blue	$350	$ 65
50c Jefferson, orange	$700	$140
$1 Perry, black, circles broken	$1,100	$375
$1, Perry, circles complete	$2,300	$750
$2 James Madison, bright blue	$3,300	$1,100
$5 John Marshall, dark green	$4,500	$2,250

WATERMARKS ADDED

As added security, the Postal Service used watermarked paper on stamps, commencing with the regular issue of 1895. The watermark chosen at first was a repetition of the double-line serif letters "USPS" (for "United States Postage Stamp") in horizontal lines covering the page. Collectors use special tools to determine if the paper contains these watermarks. On some stamps, only a portion of a letter might appear, and its detection is especially challenging.

In at least two instances, on the 6-cent and 8-cent stamps, printers used some paper intended for the production of revenue stamps and watermarked "USIR," and they are valued at many times the amounts listed here.

1895	Unused	Used
1c Franklin, blue	$8.50	$.30
2c Washington, carmine, Type I	$40	$2.50
2c, Washington, Type II	$45	$4.50
2c, Washington, Type III	$5.50	$.25
3c Jackson, purple	$42	$2
4c Lincoln, dark brown	$60	$2
5c Grant, chocolate	$52.50	$2.50

1c Franklin,
blue

2c Washington, carmine,
Type II

1895	Unused	Used
6c Garfield, dull brown	$155	$6.50
8c Sherman, violet-brown	$85	$3
10c Webster, dark green	$110	$2
15c Clay, dark blue	$250	$15
50c Jefferson, orange	$325	$40
$1 Perry, black, circles broken	$750	$100
$1, Perry circles complete	$1,500	$250
$2 Madison, bright blue	$1,300	$450
$5 John Marshall, dark green	$2,500	$675

1897-1903	Unused	Used
1c Franklin, deep green	$13	$.30
2c Washington, red, Type IV	$13.50	$.20
4c Lincoln, rose-brown	$40	$2.50
5c Grant, dark blue	$45	$1.75
6c Garfield, lake	$65	$5.50
10c Webster, brown, Type I	$250	$5
10c Webster, orange-brown, Type II	$200	$5
15c Clay, olive-green	$200	$10.50

2c Washington, carmine, Type III *3c Jackson, purple*

5c Grant, chocolate

4c Lincoln, dark brown

6c Garfield, dull brown

8c Sherman, violet-brown

10c Webster, dark green

15c Clay, dark blue

1c Franklin, deep green

4c Lincoln, rose-brown

2c Washington, red, Type III

5c Grant, dark blue

6c Garfield, lake

10c Webster, brown, Type I

15c Clay, olive-green

LOOKING WEST

Originally planned as a set of two-color stamps in conjunction with the Trans-Mississippi and International Exposition of 1898, the second commemorative set was issued in single colors because the press capacity of the BEP was needed to produce tax stamps intended to provide revenue for the Spanish-American War. While not so extensive as the Columbian set that preceded them, the Trans-Mississippi set includes some of the best-liked stamps ever issued by the United States.

1c Marquette on the Mississippi, green

1898	Unused	Used
1c Marquette on the Mississippi, green	$45	$6.25
2c Farming in the West, copper-red	$40	$2
4c Indian Hunting Buffalo, orange	$210	$35
5c Fremont on Rocky Mountains, blue	$225	$25
8c Troops Guarding Train, violet-brown	$270	$55
10c Hardships of Emigration, gray-violet	$250	$32.50
50c Western Mining Prospector, sage-green	$850	$225
$1 Western Cattle in Storm, black	$2,000	$900
$2 Mississippi River Bridge, orange-brown	$2,200	$1,300

*2c Farming in the West,
copper-red*

*4c Indian Hunting Buffalo,
orange*

5c Fremont on Rocky Mountains,
blue

8c Troops Guarding Train,
violet-brown

10c Hardships of Emigration,
gray-violet

50c Western Mining Prospector,
sage-green

$1 Western Cattle in Storm,
black

$2 Mississippi River Bridge,
orange-brown

20ᵀᴴ CENTURY PROGRESS

A commemorative set designed to support the Pan-American Exposition in Buffalo, N.Y., in 1901 again echoed the quickly dismissed definitive Pictorial Issue of 1869. Both were bi-color issues that emphasized rapid transportation. Some 1-, 2-, and 4-cent stamps were accidentally printed with their centers inverted.

The regular-issue stamps printed by the BEP (known as the "Second Bureau Issue") starting in 1902 featured portraits once again. Their ornate frames were all different. Martha Washington, the wife of the first President, became the first woman on a definitive U.S. stamp.

8c Martha Washington,
violet-black

1c Fast Lake Navigation, green and black

2c Empire State Express, carmine and black

4c Electric Auto, red-brown and black

5c Niagara Falls Bridge ultramarine and black

8c Sault Ste. Marie Locks, brown-violet and black

10c Ocean Navigation, yellow-brown and black

1901	Unused	Used
1c Fast Lake Navigation, green and black	$50	$5
2c Empire State Express, carmine and black	$35	$2
4c Electric Auto, red-brown and black	$190	$25
5c Niagara Falls Bridge, ultramarine and black	$200	$25
8c Sault Ste. Marie Locks, brown-violet and black	$220	$75
10c Ocean Navigation, yellow-brown and black	$250	$40

1902-03 Second Bureau Issue		
1c Franklin, blue-green	$14	$.20
2c Washington, carmine	$20	$.20
3c Jackson, bright violet	$70	$4
4c Grant, brown	$70	$1.90
5c Lincoln, blue	$75	$2
6c Garfield, claret	$80	$5
8c Martha Washington, violet-black	$55	$3
10c Webster, pale red-brown	$80	$2.50
13c Benjamin Harrison, purple-black	$60	$12

*1c Franklin,
blue-green*

2c Washington, carmine

3c Jackson, bright violet

4c Grant, brown

10c Webster, pale red-brown

13c Benjamin Harrison,
purple-black

15c Clay, olive-green

50c Jefferson, orange

$1 David Farragut, black

Second Bureau Issue	Unused	Used
15c Clay, olive-green	$225	$10
50c Jefferson, orange	$570	$32.50
$1 David Farragut, black	$975	$80
$2 James Madison, dark blue	$1,500	$225
$5 Marshall, dark green	$3,000	$750

(A 4-cent imperforate stamp and 1- and 2-cent coils, while collectible, are very rare and are not listed here.)

$2 James Madison, dark blue

$5 Marshall, dark green

1c Franklin, blue-green

5c Lincoln, blue

6c Garfield, claret

1906-08 Imperforate	Unused	Used
1c Franklin, blue-green	$55	$45
5c Lincoln, blue	$700	$950
2c Washington, carmine, numerous types and shades of color not listed	$8	$.20
1906 Imperforate		
2c Washington, carmine	$55	$45

2c Washington, carmine, 1903

2c Washington, carmine, 1906

EXPOS COMMEMORATED

Two sets of stamps supported the Louisiana Purchase Exposition in St. Louis, Mo., in 1904, and the Jamestown Exposition in Hampton Roads, Va., in 1907. The two expositions and the stamp sets commemorated significant events in the history of the nation and the historical figures around them, the first permanent English settlement and the agreement with France that doubled the size of the United States.

1904 Louisiana Purchase	Unused	Used
1c Robert R. Livingston, green	$60	$6.50
2c Jefferson, carmine	$50	$2.50
3c James Monroe, violet	$125	$58
5c William McKinley, dark blue	$150	$40

*2c Jefferson,
carmine*

*3c James Monroe,
violet*

1c Robert R. Livingston, green   *5c William McKinley, dark blue*

10c Map of Territory, red-brown

1904 Louisiana Purchase	Unused	Used
10c Map of Territory, red-brown	$260	$60

1c John Smith, green

2c Founding of Jamestown, carmine

5c Pocahontas, blue

1907 Jamestown	Unused	Used
1c John Smith, green	$45	$4.25
2c Founding of Jamestown, carmine	$50	$3.75
5c Pocahontas, blue	$200	$40

THE COMPLEX
WASHINGTON-FRANKLINS

The Washington-Franklin series contained: Different paper and watermarks, different perforations or no perforations, different presses that yielded different sizes, coils, errors, subtle engraving alterations, and some of the most common stamps, and some of the most rare. The "Third Bureau Issues" were at the same time the simplest and the most complex series turned out by the United States Post Office at the time. Because of its size and complexity, the series intimidates many collectors today, while others rejoice in being able to unravel each stamp's mysteries. Most, but not all, of these varieties are listed here. A beginner would be prudent to obtain an expert's certification for the more pricey stamps.

Imperforate stamps were produced for private companies who made their own coil stamps by pasting together sheets of stamps, cutting them into strips, pasting them together again and again, and finally dispensing the stamps through vending machines. The Post Office Department also produced its own coil stamps in vertical and horizontal strips.

In an attempt to better control the shrinkage of stamp paper when drying, the Bureau of Engraving and Printing experimented by adding 30 percent rag stock to the wood pulp used to make other paper. The change did not make an appreciable difference, and the experiment was dropped, but some stamps in this era are printed on the new paper, which has a slightly more gray appearance and is known in the hobby as "bluish paper."

1c Franklin,
green, ONE CENT

2c Washington,
carmine, TWO CENTS

4c Washington, orange-brown *5c Washington, blue*

6c Washington, red-orange *8c Washington, olive-green*

10c Washington, yellow

13c Washington, blue-green

15c Washington, pale ultramarine

50c Washington, violet

$1 Washington,
violet-brown

1c Franklin, green,
ONE CENT, coil

2c Washington, carmine,
TWO CENTS, coil

4c Washington,
orange-brown, coil

5c Washington,
blue, coil

1c Franklin, green,
ONE CENT, coil

2c Washington, carmine, TWO
CENTS, coil

4c Washington,
red-brown, coil

5c Washington,
blue, coil

10c Washington,
yellow

8c Franklin,
olive-bistre

12c Franklin,
claret-brown

1908-09	Unused	Used
1c Franklin, green, ONE CENT	$13	$.20
2c Washington, carmine, TWO CENTS	$11	$.20
3c Washington, deep violet, Type I, 3 CENTS	$45	$4.50
4c Washington, orange-brown	$45	$1.20
5c Washington, blue	$60	$2.50
6c Washington, red-orange	$80	$5
8c Washington, olive-green	$60	$3.50
10c Washington, yellow	$90	$2.50
13c Washington, blue-green	$70	$50
15c Washington, pale ultramarine	$85	$6.50
50c Washington, violet	$400	$30
$1 Washington, violet-brown	$575	$100

Imperforates, Double-Line Watermark		
1c Franklin, green, ONE CENT	$19	$7.50
2c Washington, carmine, TWO CENTS	$28	$5.50
3c Washington, deep violet, Type I, 3 CENTS	$70	$57.50
4c Washington, orange-brown	$89	$72.50
5c Washington, blue	$115	$90

1908-09 Coils, Double–Line Watermark, Perforation 12 Horizontally	Unused	Used
1c Franklin, green, ONE CENT	$85	$100
2c Washington, carmine, TWO CENTS	$110	$55
4c Washington, orange-brown	$315	$350
5c Washington, blue	$290	$425

1908-09 Coils, Double–Line Watermark, Perforation 12 Vertically		
1c Franklin, green, ONE CENT	$165	$250
2c Washington, carmine, TWO CENTS	$165	$325
4c Washington, orange-brown	$380	$375
5c Washington, blue	$375	$450
10c Washington, yellow	$4,800	$4,600

1909 "Bluish Paper"		
1c Franklin, green, ONE CENT	$185	$150
2c Washington, carmine, TWO CENTS	$215	$150
3c Washington, deep violet, Type I, 3 CENTS	$3,000	$5,000
6c Washington, red-orange	$2,000	$18,000
10c Washington, yellow	$2,250	$9,000

20c Franklin,
light ultramarine

30c Franklin,
orange-red

$1 Franklin,
violet-brown

9c Franklin,
salmon red

*10c
Franklin,
orange-
yellow*

*12c Franklin,
carmine*

*13c Franklin,
apple green*

15c Franklin,
gray

20c Franklin,
light ultramarine

50c Franklin,
red-violet

$1 Franklin,
violet-brown

1910-11 Single-Line Watermark Introduced	Unused	Used
1c Franklin, green, 1 CENT	$14	$.30
2c Washington, carmine, 2 CENTS	$14.75	$.30
3c Washington, deep violet, Type I	$33	$2.50
4c Washington, brown	$36.50	$1
5c Washington, blue	$42	$1
6c Washington, red-orange	$47.50	$1.30
8c Washington, olive-green	$155	$30
10c Washington, yellow	$160	$7
15c Washington, pale ultramarine	$360	$30
1910 Imperforate		
1c Washington, green	$9.50	$4
2c Washington, carmine	$15	$2.50
1910 Coil Perforation 12 Horizontally, Single-Line		
1c Washington, green	$95	$40
2c Washington, carmine	$155	$55
1910 Coil Perforation 12 Vertically		
1c Washington, green	$350	$100
2c Washington, carmine	$1,750	$600

1894 - 1931

1910 Coil Perforation 8-1/2 Horizontally	Unused	Used
1c Washington, green	$12	$10.50
2c Washington, carmine	$80	$25

1910-13 Coil Perforation 8-1/2 Vertically		
1c Washington, green	$57	$42.50
2c Washington, carmine	$80	$22.50
3c Washington, deep violet, Type I	$100	$75
4c Washington, brown	$105	$70
5c Washington, blue	$105	$70

1912-14 Single-Line Watermark, Perforation 12		
1c Washington, green	$16.75	$.20
2c Washington, carmine, Type I	$11	$.20
7c Washington, black	$110	$16

1912 Imperforate		
1c Washington, green	$2.80	$.25
2c Washington, carmine, Type I	$4	$.95

Coil Perforation 8-1/2 Horizontally		
1c Washington, green	$9	$8.75
2c Washington, carmine, Type I	$12.50	$9

Coil Perforation 8-1/2 Vertically	Unused	Used
1c Washington, green	$33	$7.50
2c Washington, carmine, Type I	$65	$1

1912-14 Single-Line, Perforation 12	Unused	Used
8c Franklin, pale olive-green	$60	$1.25
9c Franklin, salmon red	$75	$23
10c Franklin, orange-yellow	$60	$.40
12c Franklin, claret brown	$70	$4.25
15c Franklin, gray	$120	$3.50
20c Franklin, ultramarine	$250	$25
30c Franklin, orange-red	$150	$20
50c Franklin, violet	$500	$40

1912 Double-Line, Perforation 12	Unused	Used
50c Franklin, violet	$325	$38
$1 Franklin, violet-brown	$625	$100

1914-15 Single-Line Watermark, Perforation 10 (some 1c, 2c and 5c with compound perforations)	Unused	Used
1c Washington, green, ONE CENT	$6.50	$.20
2c Washington, carmine, TWO CENTS	$6	$.20

1914-15 Single-Line Watermark, Perforation 10 (some 1c, 2c and 5c with compound perforations)	Unused	Used
3c Washington, deep violet, Type I	$33	$3
4c Washington, brown	$50	$.75
5c Washington, blue	$50	$.75
6c Washington, red-orange	$55	$3
7c Washington, black	$135	$7.50
8c Washington, pale olive-green	$60	$1.50
9c Washington, salmon red	$78	$15
10c Washington, orange-yellow	$72.50	$2
11c Washington, dark green	$43	$16.50
12c Washington, claret-brown	$42.50	$6
15c Washington, gray	$170	$9.25
20c Washington, ultramarine	$265	$6
30c Washington, orange-red	$335	$22.50
50c Washington, violet	$750	$37.50
1914 Coil Stamps, Perforation 10 Horizontally		
1c Washington, green	$2.75	$1.50
2c Washington, carmine	$17.50	$18.50

Coil Perforation 10 Vertically	Unused	Used
1c Washington, green	$45.50	$8
2c Washington, carmine	$70	$2
3c Washington, deep violet, Type I	$350	$200
4c Washington, brown	$250	$85
5c Washington, blue	$72.50	$52.50

1914-16 Rotary Press Coil Stamps, Perforation 10 Horizontally		
1c Washington, green	$9	$9.50
2c Washington, red, Type I	$3,500	$475
2c Washington, carmine, Type III	$27.50	$7

Rotary Press Perforation 10 Vertically		
1c Washington, green	$22.50	$1.75
2c Washington, carmine-rose, Type I	$175	$4.50
2c Washington, red, Type II	$140	$12
2c Washington, carmine, Type III	$14	$1.50
3c Washington, deep violet, Type I	$425	$225

Rotary Press Perforation 10 Vertically		
4c Washington, brown	$55	$35
5c Washington, blue	$44	$37.50

1914 Imperforate Coil, Rotary Press	Unused	Used
2c Washington, carmine	$675	---

1915 Flat Plate Printing, on Double-Line Watermarked Paper, Perforation 10		
$1 Washington, violet-black	$1,225	$200

1915 Single-Line Watermarked Paper, Perforation 11		
2c Washington, pale carmine-red	$225	$300

1916-17 Un-Watermarked, Perforation 10, $2 and $5 Values Renewed Issue of 1902-03		
1c Washington, green	$14	$.65
2c Washington, carmine	$8	$.25
3c Washington, violet, Type I	$125	$20
4c Washington, orange-brown	$65	$2.25
5c Washington, blue	$110	$3.50
5c Washington, carmine, error	$750	---
6c Washington, red-orange	$135	$18.50
7c Washington, black	$180	$34.50
8c Washington, olive-green	$110	$10.50
9c Washington, salmon red	$125	$35
10c Washington, orange-yellow	$175	$8.50

1916-17 Un-Watermarked, Perforation 10, $2 and $5 Values Renewed Issue of 1902-03	Unused	Used
11c Washington, dark green	$68	$37.50
12c Washington, claret brown	$100	$13
15c Washington, gray	$270	$22.50
20c Washington, light ultramarine	$325	$24.50
50c Washington, light violet	$1,450	$105
$1 Washington, violet-black	$1,050	$32.50
$2 Madison, dark blue	$490	$68
$5 Marshall, light green	$390	$84

1918-20 Imperforate		
1c Washington, green	$2	$1
2c Washington, carmine	$2.50	$2.25
3c Washington, violet, Type I	$35	$22.50
3c Washington, violet, Type II	$22.50	$18.50

1916-22 Rotary Press Coil Stamps, Perforation 10 Horizontally		
1c Washington, green	$1.75	$.75
2c Washington, carmine, Type II	$35	$18
2c Washington, carmine, Type III	$6	$1.75
3c Washington, violet, Type I	$7	$1.50

Perforation 10 Vertically	Unused	Used
1c Washington, green	$1	$.25
2c Washington, carmine, Type II	$2,750	$700
2c Washington, carmine, Type III	$13.50	$.25
3c Washington, violet, Type I	$38	$3
3c vWashington, iolet, Type II	$23	$1
4c Washington, orange-brown	$25	$6
5c Washington, blue	$5	$1
10c Washington, orange-yellow	$32.50	$10.50

1917-19 Perforation 11		
1c Washington, green	$.90	$.25
2c Washington, rose, Type I	$.90	$.25
2c Washington, deep rose, Type Ia	$335	$220
3c Washington, violet, Type I	$22	$.20
3c Washington, dark violet, Type II	$25	$1.50
4c Washington, brown	$18	$.25
5c Washington, blue	$15	$.25
5c Washington, rose, error	$600	$700
6c Washington, red-orange	$16.50	$.50
7c Washington, black	$37.50	$2

1917-19 Perforation 11	Unused	Used
8c Washington, olive-bistre	$22	$1
9c Washington, salmon red	$24	$3
10c Washington, orange-yellow	$30	$.20
11c Washington, light green	$20	$5
12c Washington, claret-brown	$20	$.75
13c Washington, apple green	$23	$10
15c Washington, gray	$60.50	$1.50
20c Washington, light ultramarine	$62.50	$.50
30c Washington, orange-red	$47	$1.50
50c Washington, red-violet	$88	$.75
$1 Washington, violet-brown	$100	$2.75
Double-Line Watermark (old imp sheets of 1908-09 perforated)		
2c Washington, carmine, TWO CENTS	$600	$1,300
1918, Un-Watermarked Paper, Perforation 11		
$2 Franklin, orange-red and black	$1,250	$300
$5 Franklin, deep green and black	$425	$53
1918-20, Offset Printing, Perforation 11		
1c Washington, gray-green	$6.50	$.50
2c Washington, carmine, Type IV	$42.50	$5

1918-20, Offset Printing, Perforation 11	Unused	Used
2c Washington, carmine, Type V	$35	$1.50
2c Washington, carmine, Type Va	$17.50	$.75
2c Washington, carmine, Type VI	$72.50	$1.50
2c Washington, carmine, Type VII	$42	$.35
3c Washington, violet, Type III	$7.50	$.25
3c Washington, purple, Type IV	$2.50	$.25
1918-20 Imperforate		
1c Washington, green	$22.50	$25
2c Washington, carmine-rose, Type IV	$90	$82.50
2c Washington, carmine-rose, Type V	$375	$175
2c Washington, carmine-rose, Type Va	$37.50	$35.50
2c Washington, carmine-rose, Type VI	$110	$90
3c Washington, violet, Type IV	$19	$15
Perforation 12-1/2		
1c Washington, gray green	$42	$40
1919 Rotary Press "Coil Waste" Perforation 11 x 10 (size 19-1/2-20 mm wide x 22-22-1/4 mm high)		
1c Washington, green	$23.50	$20

1919 Rotary Press "Coil Waste" Perforation 11 x 10 (size 19-1/2-20 mm wide x 22-22-1/4 mm high)	Unused	Used
2c Washington, carmine-rose, Type III	$18.50	$15.50
3c Washington, deep violet, Type II	$75	$70

1920 Perforation 10 x 11 (size 19 x 22-1/2-22-3/4)		
1c Washington, green	$18	$1.35

1921, Perforation 10 (size 19 x 22-1/2 mm)		
1c Washington, green	$1.50	$.25

Perforation 11 (size 19-1/2-20 x 22 mm)		
1c Washington, green	$250	$220
2c Washington, carmine-rose	$145	$185

1920 Perforation 11		
$2 Franklin, carmine and black	$440	$50

*$2 Franklin,
carmine and black*

*$5 Franklin,
deep green and black*

COMMEMORATIVE VARIETIES

The three commemorative stamps issued in 1909 each had at least two varieties—perforate and imperforate. The stamp to mark the 100th anniversary of Abraham Lincoln's birth used the same frame design as the Washington-Franklin definitive series but substituted a profile of Lincoln for the vignette. It had a third variety—it was printed on the high-rag-content "Bluish paper."

There was really no postal reason to print the Alaska-Yukon-Pacific Exposition stamp in imperforate form because vending machines for the private coil stamps were not set up to handle the slightly horizontal shape of the stamp. However, one vender packaged two of the commemoratives with a 1-cent regular-issue stamp in a little envelope as a souvenir of the exposition in Seattle and sold them at face value of 5 cents.

The third commemorative issued in 1909 served double duty, celebrating two events separated by 200 years on the Hudson River in New York State. One was the discovery and exploration of the river by explorer Henry Hudson; the other was the demonstration of a steam-powered ship by Robert Fulton.

2c Lincoln,
carmine, perforate

2c Lincoln,
carmine, imperforate

2c Seward, carmine

2c Seward, carmine, imperforate

1909 Centenary of Lincoln's Birth	Unused	Used
2c Lincoln, carmine	$15	$3.50
2c Lincoln, carmine, imperforate	$60	$50
2c Lincoln, carmine, bluish paper	$300	$275

2c Hudson-Fulton, imperforate

2c Hudson-Fulton, carmine

1c Balboa, green

2c Panama Canal, carmine

Alaska-Yukon-Pacific	Unused	Used
2c Seward, carmine	$20	$3
2c Seward, carmine, imperforate	$60	$42.50
Hudson-Fulton		
2c carmine	$17.50	$6
2c carmine, imperforate	$70	$55

1913 Panama-Pacific DL Watermark Perforation 12	Unused	Used
1c Balboa, green	$38	$2.50
2c Panama Canal, carmine	$37	$1.25
5c Golden Gate, blue	$125	$12.50
10c Discovery of San Francisco, orange-yellow	$180	$40
10c Discovery of San Francisco, orange	$300	$23

5c Golden Gate, blue

10c Discovery of San Fransisco, yellow-orange

10c Discovery of San Fransisco, orange

1c Balboa , green

Perforation 10	Unused	Used
1c Balboa, green	$45	$8
2c Panama Canal, carmine	$140	$2.75
5c Golden Gate, blue	$310	$25
10c Discovery of San Francisco, orange	$1,350	$100

5c Golden Gate, blue

10c Discovery of San Fransisco, orange

3c "Victory" figure, violet

1919 Victory Flat Plate Printing, Perforation 11, Celebrated the Victory of the Allies in World War I	Unused	Used
3c "Victory" figure, violet	$19	$4.50

1920 Pilgrim Tercentenary Commemorated the Landing of the Pilgrims at Plymouth, Mass. (This set had no country designation.)		
1c Mayflower, green	$9.50	$3.75
2c Landing of the Pilgrims, carmine-rose	$12	$2.50
5c Signing of the Compact, deep blue	$65	$20

1c Mayflower, green

2c Landing of the Pilgrims, carmine-rose

5c Signing of the Compact, deep blue

PHASING OUT FLAT PLATE PRINTING

The subjects of the regular-issue series introduced in 1922 were chosen to give historical and educational interest to the stamps. These "Fourth Bureau Issues" were the last to be printed on flat-plate presses, with some exceptions, notably the low-volume $1-$5 values. The issue used three border designs for 21 values; the 15-cent Statue of Liberty had a border design of its own. Imperforate stamps were still produced for private coil venders.

In 1923 the first BEP-applied precancel was made to 1-cent stamps while on the rotary presses. Precancels (in this case, two lines within thin bars reading "NEW YORK/N.Y.") reduced handling time and had been applied previously at post offices. The first precanceled coil stamps were for New York and Chicago in 1924.

1/2c Nathan Hale, olive-brown

1c Franklin, deep green

1922-26	Unused	Used
1/2c Nathan Hale, olive-brown	$.60	$.20
1c Franklin, deep green	$4.50	$.20
1-1/2c Warren G. Harding, yellow-brown	$5.50	$.75
2c Washington, carmine	$4.50	$.20
3c Lincoln, violet	$33	$1.50
4c Martha Washington, yellow-brown	$35	$.50
5c Theodore Roosevelt, dark blue	$33.50	$.20
6c Garfield, red-orange	$55	$1.85
8c Ulysses S. Grant, olive-green	$65	$1.30
9c Jefferson, rose	$28.50	$2.25
10c Monroe, orange	$35	$.20
11c Rutherford B. Hayes, light blue	$4.25	$.45
12c Grover Cleveland, brown-violet	$15	$.50
14c American Indian, blue	$9	$2
15c Statue of Liberty, gray	$35	$.20
20c Golden Gate, carmine-rose	$40	$.20
25c Niagara Falls, yellow-green	$33.50	$1.50
30c Bison, olive-brown	$50	$.60
50c Arlington Monument, lilac	$90	$.25

1-1/2c Warren G. Harding,
yellow-brown

2c Washington,
carmine

3c Lincoln,
violet

4c Martha Washington,
yellow-brown

5c Theodore Roosevelt, dark blue

6c Garfield, red-orange

7c McKinley,
black

8c Ulysses S. Grant,
olive-green

9c Jefferson,
rose

10c Monroe,
orange

11c Rutherford B.
Hayes, light blue

12c Grover Cleveland,
brown-violet

14c American Indian, blue

15c Statue of Liberty, gray

*20c Golden Gate,
carmine-rose*

1922-26	Unused	Used
$1 Lincoln Memorial, violet-black	$70	$1.25
$2 Capitol, deep blue	$170	$11
$5 America, carmine and blue	$350	$18

25c Niagara Falls, yellow-green

30c Bison, olive-brown

50c Arlington Monument, lilac

$1 Lincoln Memorial, violet-black

$2 Capitol, deep blue

$5 America, carmine and blue

1923-25 Imperforate	Unused	Used
1c Franklin, green	$17	$8
1-1/2c Harding, yellow-brown	$3.50	$2.50
2c Washington, carmine	$3.60	$2.50

1923 Rotary Press, Perforation 11 x 10		
1c Franklin, green	$165	$200
2c Washington, carmine	$155	$200

1923-26 Perforation 10		
1c Franklin, green	$18.25	$.75
1-1/2c Harding, yellow-brown	$5	$.90
2c Washington, carmine	$3.75	$.25
3c Lincoln, violet	$33.50	$3.50
4c Martha Washington, yellow-brown	$25	$.60
5c Roosevelt, dark blue	$25	$.50
6c Garfield, red-orange	$18.50	$.90

1923-26 Perforation 10		
7c William McKinley, black	$25	$12
8c Grant, olive green	$32.50	$8.50
9c Jefferson, rose	$7.50	$5
10c Monroe, orange	$66	$.35

Perforation 11	Unused	Used
2c carmine	$425	$400
1923-29 Coils Perforation 10 Vertically		
1c green	$.60	$.20
1-1/2c brown	$1.35	$.20
2c carmine, Type I	$.50	$.20
2c carmine, Type II	$160	$12.50
3c violet	$14	$.20
4c yellow-brown	$8.50	$.75
5c dark blue	$2.95	$.35
10c Monroe, orange	$7.25	$.25
Perforation 10 Horizontally		
1c yellow-green	$.60	$.20
1-1/2c yellow-brown	$.75	$.35
2c carmine	$.65	$.40

A POPULAR MEMORIAL

The 2-cent black stamp memorial to Warren G. Harding was hurried into production after the unexpected death of the president after two years in office. It was planned to be on sale for only two months, but the stamp proved to be so popular that its sale and production was extended to five months. The stamp has four varieties: two flat-plate printings, perforation 11 and imperforate, and a perforation 10 rotary press version, along with a perforation 11 rotary press version that is very rare and valuable and is not listed here. The design of the black stamp was used for the brown 1-1/2-cent value of the 1922-25 series a year later. The Teapot Dome oil field leasing scandal led to Harding's administration being considered the most corrupt in U.S. history.

2c Harding, rotary press, perforation 10

2c Harding, black, perforation 11

2c Harding imperforate

1923	Unused	Used
2c Harding, black, perforation 11	$1.50	$.20
2c Harding, imperforate	$17.50	$11
2c Harding, rotary press, perforation 10	$27.50	$3.50

1924 Huguenot-Walloon		
1c "Nieu Nederland," green	$6.75	$5
2c Landing at Fort Orange, carmine-rose	$9.75	$3.75
5c Ribault Memorial, blue	$60	$28.50

1c "Nieu Nederland," green

2c Landing at Fort Orange, carmine-rose

Lexington-Concord	Unused	Used
1c Washington at Cambridge, green	$9	$5.95
2c "Birth of Liberty," carmine-rose	$13.50	$8
5c Minute Man, blue	$60	$21.50

Norse-American		
2c "Restaurationen," carmine and black	$10.25	$6
5c Viking ship, blue and black	$40	$23.50

1925-26		
13c Benjamin Harrison, green	$25	$.75
17c Woodrow Wilson, black	$31.50	$.50

5c Ribault Memorial,
blue

1c Washington at Cambridge,
green

*2c "Birth of Liberty,"
carmine rose*

*5c Minute Man,
blue*

*2c "Restaurationen,"
carmine and black*

*5c Viking ship,
blue and black*

13c Benjamin Harrison, green

17c Woodrow Wilson, black

THE 2-CENT REDS

The U.S. Post Office began to appreciate the value of collectible commemorative stamps when the 150-year anniversary of the Revolutionary War arrived. No longer were commemoratives issued just in sets and to support an organized exposition. Instead, single stamps were issued to commemorate a person or event and became collectible themselves. The stamps paid the first-class mail rate and were printed in the standard carmine rose specified by the Universal Postal Union for such stamps. Some, like "Molly Pitcher," the iconic heroine of the Battle of Monmouth, and the "Hawaii/1778-1928" were just black overprints on regular-issue stamps. The parade of commemorative stamps that have become known as the "2-cent Reds" lasted until a rate change in 1932.

2c Battle of Monmouth, Molly Pitcher

*2c Liberty Bell,
carmine-rose*

*2c Battle of White Plains,
carmine-rose*

*5c Ericsson
Memorial,
gray-lilac*

2c Vermont Sesquicentennial

1926 Sesquicentennial Expo	Unused	Used
2c Liberty Bell, carmine-rose	$5.75	$.80
5c Ericsson Memorial, gray-lilac	$16.50	$4.25
2c Battle of White Plains, carmine-rose	$3.75	$2.50
2c Battle of White Plains, Souvenir Sheet of 25	$750	$600

1926 Rotary Press, Imperforate	Unused	Used
1-1/2c yellow-brown	$4	$4.25
1926-34 Perforation 11 x 10-1/2		
1c green	$.50	$.20
1-1/2c yellow-brown	$3.75	$.20
2c Washington, carmine, Type I	$.40	$.20

2c Valley Forge

2c Burgoyne Campaign

2c Hawaii Sesquicentennial

5c Hawaii, blue

1926-34 Perforation 11 x 10-1/2	Unused	Used
2c Washington, carmine, Type II	$625	$15
3c Lincoln, violet	$1	$.20
4c yellow-brown	$4.25	$.30
5c dark blue	$4	$.20
6c red-orange	$6.50	$.20
7c black	$5.75	$.20
8c olive-green	$5.75	$.20
9c orange-red	$4.50	$.20
10c orange	$6.75	$.20
1927 Perforation 11		
2c Vermont Sesquicentennial	$3.25	$2.15
2c Burgoyne Campaign	$6.95	$3.95
1928		
2c Valley Forge	$2.50	$1.10
1928 Perforation 11 x 10-1/2 Rotary Press		
2c Battle of Monmouth (Molly Pitcher)	$2.50	$2.25
2c Hawaii Sesquicentennial	$7.75	$6
5c Hawaii, blue	$37.50	$25

2c International Civil Aeronautics Conference

5c International Civil Aeronautics Conference, blue

2c George Rogers Clark, carmine and black

1928 Perforation 11	Unused	Used
2c International Civil Aeronautics Conference	$4	$2.25
5c Internatl Civil Aeronautics Conference, blue	$13	$5
1929		
2c George Rogers Clark, carmine and black	$2.25	$1.10
Perforation 11 x 10-1/2 Rotary		
1/2c Hale, olive-brown	$.65	$.20
1929 Electric Light 50th Anniversary		
2c Perforation 11, flat plate	$2.25	$1.50
2c Perforation 11 x 10-1/2 Rotary	$1.50	$.45

1929 Electric Light 50th Anniversary	Unused	Used
2c Coil, perforation 10 vertically	$28.50	$2.50
1929 Perforation 11		
2c Sullivan Expedition	$1.75	$1.40

2c Electric Light, perforation 11, flat plate

2c Electric Light, perforation 11 x 10-1/2 Rotary

2c Electric Light, coil, perforation 10 vertically

2c Sullivan Expedition

BEWARE OF THE OVERPRINT

In an attempt to counteract a spate of post office robberies in Kansas and Nebraska in the 1920s, the Post Office Department marked the current regular-issue stamps with the overprints "Kans." or "Nebr.," hoping that the marked stamps would be difficult to sell in other states. The public didn't accept the overprints and thought they were used stamps or not valid for use, and the experiment was abandoned.

Today, a high percentage of these overprinted stamps in collections are considered bogus, created by counterfeiters to bilk unsuspecting collectors. Extreme caution in acquiring them would not be misplaced.

1929 Kansas Overprints	Unused	Used
1c Franklin, green	$5	$4.75
1-1/2c Harding, yellow-brown	$6.25	$5.75
2c Washington, carmine	$5.25	$1.10
3c Lincoln, violet	$40	$32.50
4c Martha Washington, yellow-brown	$50	$30
5c Teddy Roosevelt, dark blue	$25	$16

1929 Kansas Overprints	Unused	Used
6c Garfield, red-orange	$45	$32.50
7c McKinley, black	$47.25	$32.50
8c Grant, olive-green	$150	$75
9c Jefferson, orange-red	$20	$15.50
10c Monroe, orange	$42	$17.50

1c Franklin,
green

1-1/2c Harding,
yellow-brown

2c Washington, carmine

3c Lincoln, violet

9c Jefferson, orange-red

10c Monroe, orange

1929 Nebraska Overprints	Unused	Used
1c Franklin, green	$5.75	$5.75
1-1/2c Harding, yellow-brown	$5.25	$4
2c Washington, carmine	$5.50	$1.25
3c Lincoln, violet	$24.50	$19.50
4c Martha Washington, yellow-brown	$37	$18.50
5c Teddy Roosevelt, dark blue	$33.50	$24.50
6c Garfield, red-orange	$83.50	$30
7c McKinley, black	$50	$32.50
8c Grant, olive-green	$67	$50
9c Jefferson, orange-red	$80	$50
10c Monroe, orange	$157.50	$47.50

*4c Martha Washington
yellow-brown*

*5c Teddy Roosevelt,
dark blue*

6c Garfield, red-orange

7c McKinley, black

8c Grant, olive-green

2c Battle of Fallen Timbers

1929 Perforation 11	Unused	Used
2c Battle of Fallen Timbers	$2.50	$1.50
2c Ohio River Canalization	$1.50	$1.10
1930		
2c Massachusetts Bay Colony	$1.50	$1
2c Carolina-Charleston	$2.75	$2.50
1930 Perforation 11 x 10-1/2 Rotary		
1-1/2c brown	$.85	$.20
4c William H. Taft, brown	$1.50	$.20

2c Massachusetts Bay Colony

2c Carolina-Charleston

Coil, Perforation 10 Vertically	Unused	Used
1-1/2c brown	$2.95	$.20
4c brown	$4.75	$.75

1930 Perforation 11		
2c Battle of Braddock's Field	$1.95	$1.80
2c Gen. von Steuben	$1.10	$.90

1931		
2c Gen. Casimir Pulaski	$.75	$.40

1-1/2c Harding, brown

4c William H. Taft, brown

1931 Perforation 11 x 10-1/2 Rotary	Unused	Used
11c Hayes, light blue	$5.50	$.20
12c Cleveland, brown-violet	$11.25	$.25
13c Harrison, yellow-green	$4	$.40
14c American Indian, blue	$10.50	$1.65

1931 Perforation 11 x 10-1/2 Rotary		
15c Statue of Liberty, gray	$17	$.20

Perforation 10-1/2 x 11		
17c Wilson, black	$13	$.40
20c Golden Gate, carmine-rose	$15.50	$.20
25c Niagara Falls, yellow-green	$16.25	$.20
30c Bison, olive-brown	$38	$.20
50c Arlington Monument, lilac	$67	$.20

1931 Perforation 11, Flat Plate Printing		
2c Red Cross, black and carmine-rose	$.50	$.25
2c Yorktown, carmine-rose and black	$.60	$.50

2c Battle of Braddock's Field

2c Gen. von Steuben

2c Gen. Casimir Pulaski

2c Yorktown, carmine-rose and black

1932-1954

AN EXPLOSION OF COLLECTIBLES

For the 1932 bicentennial of George Washington's birth, the post office issued a popular set of 12 stamps that featured portraits of the "Father of His Country" from a young man to his 60s.

The next year James A. Farley, who managed Franklin Roosevelt's successful presidential campaign, was given the plum cabinet post of Postmaster General and set about ingratiating himself. Both he and his boss were stamp collectors. Farley began to make a practice of autographing imperforate sheets of newly printed stamps and presenting them to his family and political cronies, in effect creating rare varieties of the stamps. When the news media calculated that Farley had given out stamps with a possible retail value of $3 million, public outrage at what became known as "Farley's Follies" forced the post office to print a new supply of the imperforate and un-gummed stamps and make them available to the public. They are all collectible in many forms today.

Single stamps from these special printings can be indistinguishable from some of their earlier printings, except for specific printed guidelines or gutters. They are relatively inexpensive, but collectors should obtain them in the proper form.

A beautifully engraved set of 10 stamps with scenes of America's National Parks was included in these imperforate sheets, and individual Parks stamps appeared on other souvenir sheets produced for stamp shows.

A new definitive set (the Fifth Bureau Issue) that appeared in 1938 featured all the U.S. presidents through Calvin Coolidge, in order of their service—as well as Martha Washington and the White House. The elegantly and simply designed set ran for 16 years and helped many young collectors learn their presidential succession for American history classes.

In 1940 a set of 36 stamps was issued to honor famous Americans who were prominent in many fields.

For patriotic, philatelic or political causes, the stamps rolled out of Washington, and many collectors consider this the golden age of the hobby.

The President, "stamp collector-in-chief," actually drew rough designs of some commemoratives he wanted the Post Office Department to issue. The day Roosevelt died, April 12, 1945, the postmaster general added "Franklin D. Roosevelt" to the United Nations commemorative stamp FDR had approved that day. The stamp was issued on April 25.

1932 Washington Bicentennial	Unused	Used
1/2c Washington, olive-brown	$.35	$.20
1c Washington, green	$.40	$.20
1-1/2c Washington, brown	$.75	$.25
2c Washington, carmine-rose	$.40	$.20
3c Washington, deep violet	$1.15	$.20
4c Washington, light brown	$.75	$.25
5c Washington, blue	$4.50	$.25
6c Washington, red-orange	$8.50	$.20
7c Washington, black	$.95	$.60
8c Washington, olive-bistre	$10	$2
9c Washington, pale red	$7.15	$.40
10c Washington, orange-yellow	$25	$.20
1932		
2c Winter Olympics, carmine-rose, perforation 11	$.95	$.40
2c Arbor Day, carmine-rose, perforation 11 x 10-1/2 rotary press	$.40	$.20
3c Olympic Games, violet, perforation 11 x 10-1/2 rotary press	$4.50	$.20
5c Olympic Games, blue perforation 11 x 10-1/2 rotary press	$6.50	$.50
3c Washington, deep violet	$.50	$.20

*1/2c Washington,
olive-brown*

*1c green Washington,
green*

*1-1/2c Washington,
brown*

*2c Washington,
carmine-rose*

*3c Washington
deep violet*

*4c Washington,
light brown*

*5c Washington,
blue*

*6c Washington,
red-orange*

*7c Washington,
black*

8c Washington,
olive-bistre

9c Washington,
pale red

10c Washington,
orange-yellow

2c Winter Olympics,
carmine-rose

2c Arbor Day,
carmine-rose

3c Olympic Games,
violet

5c Olympic Games,
blue

3c Washington,
deep violet

1932	Unused	Used
3c Washington, deep violet, coil perforation 10 vertically	$3.75	$.20
6c Garfield, deep orange	$18	$.30
3c Washington, deep violet, perforation 10 horizontally	$2.95	$.65
1932-33 Perforation 11		
3c William Penn, violet, 10-1/2 x 11	$1.10	$.30
3c Daniel Webster, violet	$1.30	$.40
3c Georgia Bicentennial, violet	$1.45	$.30
1933 Perforation		
3c Peace of 1783, violet	$.50	$.20
1c Century of Progress, yellow-green	$.60	$.20
3c Federal Building, violet	$.80	$.20
American Philatelic Society Souvenir Sheets, Imperforate, Flat Plate Printing		
1c Fort Dearborn, yellow-green	$1.50	$.95
1c Fort Dearborn, sheet of 25	$47.50	$47.50
3c Federal Building, violet	$1.50	$.95
3c Federal Buidling, sheet of 25	$38.50	$38.50
1933		
3c National Recovery Act, violet	$.40	$.20

1934	Unused	Used
3c Byrd Antarctic Expedition, dark blue	$1.65	$1.25
3c Gen. Tadeusz Kosciuszko, blue	$1.75	$1.50

1934 National Stamp Exhibition Souvenir Sheet, Imperforate		
3c Byrd Antarctic, dark blue	$5	$3
3c Byrd Antarctic, sheet of 6	$32.50	$27.50
3c Maryland Tercentenary, carmine-rose	$.60	$.30

Perforation 11 x 10-1/2, Rotary Press		
3c Mothers of America, deep violet	$.50	$.20

Perforation 11, Flat Plate Printing		
3c Mothers of America, violet	$.60	$.20
3c Wisconsin Tercentenary, deep violet	$.60	$.20

National Parks		
1c Yosemite, green	$.30	$.20
2c Grand Canyon, red	$.30	$.20
3c Mt. Rainier, deep violet	$.50	$.20
4c Mesa Verde, brown	$.50	$.40
5c Yellowstone, blue	$2	$1.35
6c Crater Lake, dark blue	$3.35	$1.95

3c William Penn,
violet

3c Daniel Webster,
violet

3c Georgia
Bicentennial, violet

3c Peace of 1783, violet

1c Century of Progress,
yellow-green

3c Federal Building, violet

3c National Recovery Act,
violet

National Parks	Unused	Used
7c Acadia, black	$1.75	$1.65
8c Zion, sage-green	$4.50	$3.65
9c Glacier, red-orange	$4.25	$1.30
10c Great Smoky Mountains, gray-black	$7.25	$2

American Philatelic Society Convention Souvenir Sheet, Imperforate		
3c Mt. Rainier, deep violet	$8.50	$4.75
3c Mt. Rainier, sheet of 6	$75	$67.50

Trans-Mississippi Philatelic Exposition Souvenir Sheet, Imperforate		
1c Yosemite, green	$3.50	$2
1c Yosemite, sheet of 6	$24.50	$20

1935 Special Printings Without Gum, Perforation 10-1/2 x 11, Rotary Press		
3c Peace of 1783, violet	$.45	$.40

Perforation 11, Flat Plate Printing		
3c Byrd Antarctic, dark blue	$1.35	$1.15

Imperforate		
3c Mothers of America, deep violet	$1.85	$1.50
3c Wisconsin, deep violet	$2	$1.25

Imperforate	Unused	Used
1c Yosemite, green	$.50	$.45
2c Grand Canyon, red	$.75	$.50
3c Mt. Rainier, deep violet	$1.25	$1.25
4c Mesa Verde, brown	$3	$2.60
5c Yellowstone, blue	$4.25	$2.50
6c Crater Lake, dark blue	$5	$4.25
7c Acadia, black	$4.25	$2.50
8c Zion, sage-green	$4.25	$3.50
9c Glacier, red-orange	$5.50	$4.75
10c Great Smoky Mountains, gray-black	$8.25	$5.50
16c Airpost special delivery, blue	$5.50	$4.50

Souvenir Sheet Special Printings		
1c Fort Dearborn, yellow-green, pane of 25	$52.50	$45
3c Federal Building, violet, pane of 25	$45	$35
3c Byrd Antarctic, dark blue, pane of 6	$35	$30
1c Yosemite, green, pane of 6	$21	$18
3c Mt. Rainier, violet, page of 6	$65	$58

1935 Perforation 11 x 10-1/2 or Perforation 11		
3c Connecticut Tercentenary, violet	$.90	$.20

*3c Byrd Antarctic Expedition,
dark blue*

*3c Gen. Tadeusz Kosciuszko,
blue*

3c Byrd Antarctic, dark blue sheet of 6

3c Maryland Tercentenary,
carmine-rose

3c Mothers of America, violet

3c Wisconsin Tercentenary,
deep violet

1c
Yosemite,
green

5c
Yellowstone,
blue

2c Grand Canyon, red

3c Mt. Rainier, deep violet

4c Mesa Verde, brown

6c Crater Lake, dark blue

7c Acadia, black

9c Glacier, red-orange

8c Zion, sage-green

1935	Unused	Used
3c California Pacific Exposition, purple	$.60	$.20
3c Boulder Dam, purple, perforation 11	$.50	$.20
3c Michigan Centenary, purple, perforation 11 x 10-1/2	$.70	$.20
1936		
3c Texas Centenary, purple	$.70	$.20
3c Rhode Island Tercentenary, purple	$.75	$.20
Third International Philatelic Exhibition souvenir sheet, imperforate	$4.50	$4
3c Connecticut, imperforate, purple	$1	$1
3c California, imperforate, purple	$1	$1
3c Michigan, imperforate, purple	$1	$1
3c Texas, imperforate, purple	$1	$1
3c Arkansas Centennial, purple	$.50	$.20
3c Oregon Territory, purple	$.40	$.20
3c Susan B. Anthony, dark violet	$.50	$.20
1936-37 Army-Navy		
1c Washington, green	$.65	$.20
2c Jackson, carmine	$.65	$.20
3c Sherman, purple	$1.25	$.20

1936-37 Army-Navy	Unused	Used
4c Lee, gray	$1.25	$.50
5c West Point, ultramarine	$1.40	$.50
1c Jones, green	$.30	$.20
2c Decatur, carmine	$.45	$.20
3c Farragut, purple	$.65	$.20
4c Sampson, gray	$1.50	$.50
5c Naval Academy Seal, ultramarine	$2	$.50
1937		
3c Northwest Territory, red-violet	$1.25	$.20
5c Virginia Dare, gray-blue	$.80	$.40
Society of Philatelic Americans Convention, souvenir sheet		
10c Great Smoky Mountains, blue-green	$1.75	$1
3c Constitution Sesquicentennial, red-violet	$2	$.20
3c Hawaii, red-violet	$.75	$.20
3c Alaska, red-violet	$.85	$.20
3c Puerto Rico, red-violet	$.85	$.20
3c Virgin Islands, red-violet	$.85	$.20

10c Great Smoky Mountains, gray-black

3c Connecticut Tercentenary, violet

3c California Pacific Exposition, purple

3c Michigan Centenary, purple

3c Texas Centenary, purple

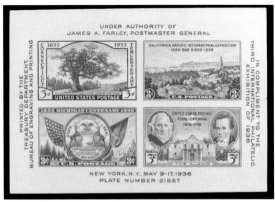

Third International Philatelic Exhibition souvenir sheet, imperforate

3c Boulder Dam, purple

3c Rhode Island Tercentenary, purple

3c Arkansas Centennial, purple

3c Oregon Territory, purple

3c Susan B. Anthony, dark violet

1c Washington, green

2c Jackson, carmine

3c Sherman, purple

1938-54 Presidential Series	Unused	Used
1/2c Ben Franklin, deep orange	$.30	$.20
1c George Washington, green	$.30	$.20
1-1/2c Martha Washington, bistre-brown	$.30	$.20
2c John Adams, rose-carmine	$.30	$.20
3c Thomas Jefferson, deep violet	$.35	$.20
4c James Madison, red-violet	$2	$.20
4-1/2c White House, dark gray	$.60	$.20
5c James Monroe, bright blue	$1	$.20
6c John Quincy Adams, red-orange	$1	$.20
7c Andrew Jackson, sepia	$1	$.20
8c Martin Van Buren, olive-green	$1	$.20
9c William H. Harrison, rose-pink	$.90	$.20
10c John Tyler, brown-red	$.90	$.20
11c James K. Polk, ultramarine	$1.50	$.20
12c Zachary Taylor, bright violet	$3	$.20
13c Millard Fillmore, blue-green	$2.95	$.20
14c Franklin Pierce, blue	$3	$.20
15c James Buchanan, blue-gray	$1.20	$.20

4c Lee, gray

5c West Point, ultramarine

1c Jones, green

2c Decatur, carmine

3c Farragut, purple

4c Sampson, gray

*5c Naval Academy Seal,
ultramarine*

*3c Northwest Territory,
red-violet*

5c Virginia Dare, gray-blue

*Society of Philatelic Americans
Convention, souvenir sheet*

*3c
Hawaii,
violet*

3c Constitution Sesquicentennial,
red-violet

3c Alaska,
violet

3c Puerto Rico,
light red-violet

3c Virgin Islands,
violet

1/2c Ben Franklin,
deep orange

1c George Washington,
green

1-1/2c Martha
Washington,
bistre-brown

1938-54 Presidential Series	Unused	Used
16c Abraham Lincoln, black	$3	$.85
17c Andrew Johnson, rose-red	$2.95	$.30
18c Ulysses S. Grant, brown-carmine	$3.95	$.25
19c Rutherford B. Hayes, bright violet	$3.95	$1.10
20c James Garfield, bright blue-green	$1.90	$.20
21c Chester Arthur, dull blue	$3.95	$.35
22c Grover Cleveland, vermilion	$3.15	$1.50
24c Benjamin Harrison, gray-black	$9.75	$.30
25c William McKinley, deep red-lilac	$2.35	$.20
30c Theodore Roosevelt, deep ultramarine	$13.50	$.20
50c William Howard Taft, light red-violet	$17.50	$.20
$1 Woodrow Wilson, purple and black	$21.50	$.20
$2 Warren Harding, yellow-green and black	$35	$6.95
$5 Calvin Coolidge, carmine and black	$175	$5.95
1938		
3c Constitution Ratification, deep violet	$1.50	$.20
3c Swedish-Finnish Tercentenary, red-violet	$.50	$.20
3c Northwest Territory, bright violet	$.65	$.20
3c Iowa Territory, violet	$.80	$.20

3c Thomas Jefferson,
deep violet

4c James Madison,
red-violet

4-1/2c White House,
dark gray

5c James Monroe,
bright blue

6c John Quincy Adams,
red-orange

7c Andrew Jackson,
sepia

8c Martin Van Buren,
olive-green

9c William H. Harrison,
rose-pink

10c John Tyler,
brown-red

*11c James K. Polk,
ultramarine*

*12c Zachary Taylor,
bright violet*

*13c Millard Fillmore,
blue-green*

*14c Franklin Pierce,
blue*

*15c James Buchanan,
blue-gray*

*16c Abraham Lincoln,
black*

*17c Andrew Johnson,
rose-red*

*18c Ulysses S. Grant,
brown-carmine*

*19c Rutherford B.
Hayes, bright violet*

*20c James Garfield,
bright blue-green*

*21c Chester Arthur,
dull blue*

*22c Grover Cleveland,
vermilion*

*24c Benjamin Harrison,
gray-black*

*25c William McKinley,
deep red-lilac*

*30c Theodore Roosevelt,
deep ultramarine*

*50c William Howard
Taft, light red-violet*

*$1 Woodrow Wilson,
purple and black*

*$2 Warren Harding,
yellow-green and black*

1939 Presidential Coils, Perforation 10 Vertically	Unused	Used
1c George Washington, green	$.60	$.20
1-1/2c Martha Washington, bistre-brown	$.75	$.20
2c John Adams, rose-carmine	$.60	$.20
3c Jefferson, deep violet	$1	$.20
4c Madison, red-violet	$11	$.50
4-1/2c White House, dark gray	$1.10	$.75
5c Monroe, bright blue	$8.25	$.50
6c John Q. Adams, red-orange	$2.50	$.30
10c Tyler, brown-red	$18	$1.10
1939 Presidential Coils, Perforation 10, Horizontally		
1c George Washington, green	$1.50	$.25
1-1/2c Martha Washington, bistre-brown	$2.75	$.90
2c John Adams, rose-carmine	$4.25	$.90
3c Jefferson, deep violet	$4.25	$3.95
1939		
3c Golden Gate Int'l Expo, bright purple	$.50	$.20
3c New York World's Fair, deep purple	$.40	$.20
3c Washington's Inauguration, red-violet	$1.50	$.20

$5 Calvin Coolidge, carmine and black

3c Washington's Inauguration, red-violet

3c New York World's Fair, deep purple

3c Baseball Centenary, violet

1c Washington Irving, bright blue-green

2c James Fennimore Cooper, rose-carmine

3c Ralph Waldo Emerson, bright red-violet

5c Louisa May Alcott, ultramarine

10c Samuel L. Clemens, dark brown

1c Henry W. Longfellow, bright blue-green

5c Walt Whitman, ultramarine

10c Booker T. Washington, dark brown

5c Dr. Walter Reed, ultramarine

3c Augustus Saint-Gaudens, bright red-violet

10c Frederic Remington, dark brown

1c Eli Whitney, bright blue-green

2c Samuel F.B. Morse, rose-carmine

5c Elias Howe, ultramarine

10c Alexander Graham Bell, dark brown

1c National Defense, Statue, green

3c Pony Express

1939	Unused	Used
3c Baseball Centenary, violet	$3.75	$.30
3c Panama Canal, deep red-violet	$.50	$.20
3c Printing Tercentenary, violet	$.40	$.20
3c Anniversary of Statehood, rose-violet	$.50	$.20

1940 Famous Americans—Authors, Poets, Educators, Scientists, Composers, Artists, Inventors	Unused	Used
1c Washington Irving, bright blue-green	$.45	$.20
2c James Fennimore Cooper, rose-carmine	$.55	$.20
3c Ralph Waldo Emerson, bright red-violet	$.55	$.20
5c Louisa May Alcott, ultramarine	$.95	$.75
10c Samuel L. Clemens, dark brown	$4.50	$3.50
1c Henry W. Longfellow, bright blue-green	$.55	$.20
2c John Greenleaf Whittier, rose-carmine	$.50	$.20
3c James Russell Lowell, bright red-violet	$.45	$.20
5c Walt Whitman, ultramarine	$1.35	$.40
10c James Whitcomb Riley, dark brown	$5.75	$4
1c Horace Mann, bright blue-green	$.30	$.25
2c Mark Hopkins, rose-carmine	$.35	$.20
3c Charles W. Eliot, bright red-violet	$.45	$.20
5c Frances E. Willard, ultramarine	$1.10	$.45
10c Booker T. Washington, dark brown	$5	$2.50
1c John James Audubon, bright blue-green	$.30	$.20
2c Dr. Crawford W. Long, rose-carmine	$.30	$.20

1940 Famous Americans—Authors, Poets, Educators, Scientists, Composers, Artists, Inventors	Unused	Used
3c Luther Burbank, bright red-violet	$.50	$.20
5c Dr. Walter Reed, ultramarine	$.60	$.35
10c Jane Addams, dark brown	$4	$3
1c Stephen Collins Foster, bright blue-green	$.40	$.20
2c John Philip Sousa, rose-carmine	$.35	$.20
3c Victor Herbert, bright red-violet	$.40	$.20
5c Edward A. MacDowell, ultramarine	$1.10	$.40
10c Ethelbert Nevin, dark brown	$9.50	$2.95
1c Gilbert Charles Stewart, bright blue-green	$.60	$.20
2c James A. McNeill Whistler, rose-carmine	$.30	$.20
3c Augustus Saint-Gaudens, bright red-violet	$.60	$.20
5c Daniel Chester French, ultramarine	$3	$.35
10c Frederic Remington, dark brown	$5	$2.75
1c Eli Whitney, bright blue-green	$1	$.35
2c Samuel F.B. Morse, rose-carmine	$.60	$.20
3c Cyrus Hall McCormick, bright red-violet	$1	$.20
5c Elias Howe, ultramarine	$2.75	$.65
10c Alexander Graham Bell, dark brown	$27.50	$4.25

1940	Unused	Used
3c Pony Express	$.80	$.20
3c Pan American Union	$.70	$.20
3c Idaho Statehood	$.60	$.20
3c Wyoming Statehood	$.70	$.20
3c Coronado Expedition	$.60	$.20
1c National Defense, Statue, green	$.40	$.20
2c National Defense, Gun, carmine	$.40	$.20
3c National Defense, torch, violet	$.40	$.20
3c Emancipation	$.75	$.55
1941		
3c Vermont Statehood	$.80	$.20
1942		
3c Kentucky Statehood	$.50	$.25
3c Win the War	$.40	$.20
5c China Resistance	$2.25	$1.75
1943		
3c Allied Nations	$.35	$.20
3c Four Freedoms	$.30	$.20

2c National Defense,
Gun, carmine

3c National Defense,
torch, violet

3c Emancipation

5c China Resistance

A PRIVATE PRINTER RETURNS

It had been 50 years since American Bank Note Co. had printed a United States stamp, but the private printing firm possessed a technology that the Bureau of Engraving and Printing did not—the ability to print more than one

5c Poland

5c Czechoslovakia

5c Norway

5c France

color. The post office wanted to show support for 13 nations occupied in the war in Europe and Asia. The set, known as the Overrun Countries Issue, features full-color depictions of the flags of the occupied nations printed in offset while frames and shading lines were engraved. Printing anomalies are known but are not listed here.

5c Greece

5c Yugoslavia

5c Albania

5c Korea

1943-44 Overrun Countries	Unused	Used
5c Poland	$.55	$.30
5c Czechoslovakia	$.50	$.20
5c Norway	$.40	$.20
5c Luxembourg	$.40	$.20
5c Netherlands	$.40	$.20
5c Belgium	$.40	$.20
5c France	$.60	$.20
5c Greece	$1.45	$.75
5c Yugoslavia	$1	$.60
5c Albania	$1.10	$.50
5c Austria	$.55	$.40
5c Denmark	$1	$.60
5c Korea	$.60	$.40
1944		
3c Transcontinental Railroad	$.45	$.30
3c Steamship Savannah	$.60	$.30
3c Telegraph	$.60	$.25
3c Corregidor	$.50	$.30
3c Motion Pictures	$.50	$.25

1945	Unused	Used
3c Florida Statehood	$.50	$.20
3c U.N. Conference	$.50	$.20
3c Marines, Iwo Jima	$.70	$.20

1945-46 Franklin D. Roosevelt Issue		
1c F.D.R., Hyde Park, blue-green	$.25	$.20
2c F.D.R., Little White House, carmine	$.35	$.20
3c F.D.R., White House, purple	$.40	$.20
5c F.D.R., Globe, bright blue	$.45	$.20
3c Army, Arch of Triumph	$.40	$.20
3c Navy, Sailors	$.50	$.20
3c Coast Guard, Landing Craft	$.40	$.20
3c Alfred E. Smith	$.45	$.20
3c Texas Statehood	$.50	$.20

1946		
3c Merchant Marine, Liberty Ship	$.40	$.20
3c Honorable Discharge Emblem	$.40	$.20
3c Tennessee Statehood	$.90	$.20
3c Iowa Statehood	$.50	$.20

1946	Unused	Used
3c Smithsonian Institution	$.40	$.20
3c Kearney Expedition	$.40	$.20
1947		
3c Thomas Alva Edison	$.50	$.20
3c Joseph Pulitzer	$.50	$.20

100 YEARS OF STAMPS

To celebrate the centenary of postage stamps in the United States, the Post Office Department produced two postal products. The first was a 3-cent blue stamp jammed with the images of George Washington and Benjamin Franklin as on the first two U.S. stamps and also representations of advances in transportation and mail carrying. (The automobile was a significant omission.)

The second was a classy souvenir sheet "in compliment to the Centenary International Philatelic Exhibition," on which were reproduced the first two stamps in different colors—the 5-cent Franklin in blue and the 10-cent Washington in a brown-orange. Each was valid for postage and remains so today.

1947	Unused	Used
3c Postage Stamp Centenary	$.40	$.20
5c Franklin/10c Washington CIPEX souvenir sheet	$2.25	$1.25
5c Franklin, blue	$1.10	$.75
10c Washington, brown-orange	$1.10	$.75
3c Doctors	$.40	$.20
3c Utah Settlement	$.40	$.20
3c U.S. Frigate Constitution	$.40	$.20
3c Everglades National Park	$.60	$.20

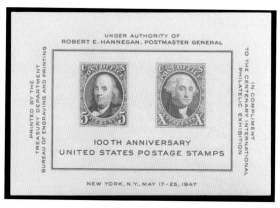

CIPEX souvenir sheet

1948	Unused	Used
3c George Washington Carver	$.75	$.20
3c California Gold	$.65	$.20
3c Mississippi Territory	$.70	$.20
3c Four Chaplains	$.80	$.20
3c Wisconsin Statehood	$.70	$.20
3c Swedish Pioneers	$.40	$.20
3c Progress of Women	$.60	$.20
3c William Allen White	$.50	$.20
3c U.S.-Canada Friendship	$.50	$.20
3c Francis Scott Key	$.60	$.20
3c Salute to Youth	$.50	$.20
3c Oregon Territory	$.70	$.20
3c Harlan F. Stone	$.60	$.20
3c Palomar Mountain Observatory	$.50	$.20
3c Clara Barton, Red Cross	$.50	$.20
3c Poultry Industry	$.75	$.20
3c Gold Star Mothers	$.50	$.20
3c Fort Kearney	$.60	$.20
3c Volunteer Firemen	$.80	$.20
3c Indian Centennial	$.70	$.20
3c Rough Riders	$.70	$.20
3c Juliette Low, Girl Scouts	$.80	$.20
3c Will Rogers	$.70	$.20

1948	Unused	Used
3c Fort Bliss	$.70	$.20
3c Moina Michael, Poppy	$.80	$.20
3c Gettysburg Address	$.80	$.20
3c American Turners	$.55	$.20
3c Joel Chandler Harris	$.80	$.20

1949		
3c Minnesota Territory	$.50	$.20
3c Washington & Lee University	$.60	$.20
3c Puerto Rico Election	$.40	$.20
3c Annapolis Tercentenary	$.45	$.20
3c Grand Army of the Republic	$.40	$.20
3c Edger Allan Poe	$.60	$.20

1950		
3c American Bankers Association	$.60	$.20
3c Samuel Gompers	$.40	$.20
National Capitol Sesquicentennial 3c Statue of "Freedom"	$.40	$.20
3c White House	$.50	$.20
3c Supreme Court	$.50	$.20
3c U.S. Capitol	$.40	$.20
3c Railroad Engineers	$.50	$.20

1950	Unused	Used
3c Kansas City, Mo.	$.50	$.20
3c Boy Scouts	$.60	$.20
3c Indiana Territory	$.60	$.20
3c California Statehood	$.60	$.20
1951		
3c United Confederate Veterans	$.50	$.20
3c Nevada Centenary	$.40	$.20
3c Landing of Cadillac, Detroit	$.40	$.20
3c Colorado Statehood	$.40	$.20
3c American Chemical Society	$.50	$.20
3c Battle of Brooklyn	$.40	$.20
1952		
3c Betsy Ross	$.50	$.20
3c 4-H Clubs	$.60	$.20
3c B. & O. Railroad	$.50	$.20
3c American Automobile Association	$.50	$.20
3c NATO	$.40	$.20
3c Grand Coulee Dam	$.40	$.20
3c Marquis de Lafayette	$.45	$.20

1952	Unused	Used
3c Mt. Rushmore Memorial	$.60	$.20
3c Engineering	$.60	$.20
3c Women in the Armed Forces	$.50	$.20
3c Gutenberg Bible	$.40	$.20
3c Newspaper Boys	$.45	$.20
3c Red Cross	$.45	$.20

1953		
3c National Guard	$.40	$.20
3c Ohio Statehood	$.50	$.20
3c Washington Territory	$.40	$.20
3c Louisiana Purchase	$.50	$.20
5c Opening of Japan Centennial	$.65	$.20
3c American Bar Association	$.60	$.20
3c Sagamore Hill	$.45	$.20
3c Future Farmers of America	$.40	$.20
3c Trucking Industry	$.40	$.20
3c Gen. George C. Patton	$.40	$.20
3c New York City Tercentenary	$.50	$.20
3c Gadsden Purchase	$.40	$.20

1954	Unused	Used
3c Columbia University Bicentennial	$.45	$.20
3c Nebraska Territory	$.40	$.20
3c Kansas Territory	$.40	$.20
3c George Eastman	$.45	$.20
3c Lewis & Clark	$.60	$.20

3c Edgar Allan Poe

3c Betsy Ross

3c Mt. Rushmore Memorial

1955-1961

VARIETIES BECOME THE NORM

The regular-issue series of 1954-68 was a precursor of things to come as the Post Office Department experimented with production methods. Many collectors specialize in the 28 denominations of the set, separating wet and dry printings, small and large holes in the perforations and phosphorescent tagging, a mail-handling innovation introduced in 1963. A specialized catalog should be consulted to determine all the varieties.

The commonly accepted name for this sixth Bureau issue, the Liberty Series, stuck because the 3-cent purple Statue of Liberty stamp inaugurated the series. Liberty also appeared in two 8-cent stamps (flat-plate printing and one two-tenths of a millimeter taller on rotary press and a re-drawn design in which the torch is below the "U.S. Postage" lettering) and an 11-cent stamp—in addition to a 3-cent coil and larger-scale imperforate varieties of the 3-cent and 8-cent Statue of Liberty stamps on a souvenir sheet of 1956.

1954-68	Unused	Used
1/2c Benjamin Franklin, red-orange	$.20	$.20
1c George Washington, dark green	$.30	$.20
1-1/4c Palace of the Governors, turquoise	$.20	$.20
1-1/2c Mount Vernon, brown-carmine	$.30	$.20
2c Thomas Jefferson, carmine-rose	$.30	$.20
2-1/2c Bunker Hill Monument, gray-blue	$.30	$.20
3c Statue of Liberty, deep violet	$.30	$.20
4c Abraham Lincoln, red-violet	$.40	$.20
4-1/2c Hermitage, blue-green	$.40	$.20
5c James Monroe, deep blue	$.45	$.20
6c Theodore Roosevelt, carmine	$1	$.20
7c Woodrow Wilson, rose-carmine	$.45	$.20
8c Statue of Liberty, violet-blue and carmine, (torch reaches margin, 22.7 mm high)	$.50	$.20
8c Statue of Liberty, Rotary press, 22.9 mm high	$.60	$.50
8c Statue of Liberty, re-drawn (torch below "postage")	$.60	$.20
8c Gen. John J. Pershing, brown	$.55	$.20
9c Alamo, rose-lilac	$.60	$.20
10c Independence Hall, rose-lake	$.65	$.20
11c Statue of Liberty, carmine and violet-blue	$.65	$.20

1954-68	Unused	Used
12c Benjamin Harrison, red	$.80	$.20
15c John Jay, rose-lake	$1.20	$.20
20c Monticello, ultramarine	$1.50	$.20
25c Paul Revere, green	$3.95	$.20
30c Robert E. Lee, black	$3.75	$.20
40c John Marshall, brown-red	$4.75	$.20
50c Susan B. Anthony, bright purple	$5.50	$.20
$1 Patrick Henry, purple	$10	$.20
$5 Alexander Hamilton, black	$120	$16.95
Coils		
1c Washington, dark green, vertically	$.60	$.20
1-1/4c Palace of the Governors, turquoise, horizontally	$.50	$.25
2c Thomas Jefferson, carmine-rose, vertically	$.20	$.20
2-1/2c Bunker Hill Monument, gray-blue, vertically	$.85	$.80
3c Statue of Liberty, deep violet, vertically	$.30	$.20
4c Abraham Lincoln, red-violet, vertically	$.30	$.20
4-1/2c Hermitage, blue-green, horizontally	$3.95	$2.75
25c Paul Revere, green, vertically	$1.70	$.45

*3c Statue of Liberty,
deep violet*

*8c Statue of Liberty, violet-blue
and carmine, (torch reaches
margin, 22.7 mm high)*

*8c Statue of Liberty, re-drawn
(torch below "postage")*

*11c Statue of Liberty,
carmine and violet blue*

1955	Unused	Used
3c Pennsylvania Academy	$.80	$.20
3c Land Grant Colleges	$.50	$.20
3c Rotary International	$1.10	$.20
3c Armed Forces Reserve	$.60	$.20
3c New Hampshire	$.65	$.20
3c Soo Locks	$.60	$.20
3c Atoms for Peace	$.50	$.20
3c Fort Ticonderoga	$.80	$.20
3c Andrew Mellon	$.80	$.20
1956		
3c Benjamin Franklin	$.60	$.20
3c Booker T. Washington	$.80	$.20
FIPEX souvenir sheet	$4.95	$4
3c Statue of Liberty, imperforate	$2.50	$2
8c Statue of Liberty, imperforate	$2.50	$2
3c FIPEX	$.40	$.20
3c Wildlife Conservation, Wild Turkey	$.40	$.20
3c Pronghorn Antelope	$.40	$.20

3c FIPEX

1956	Unused	Used
3c King Salmon	$.40	$.20
3c Pure Food & Drug Act	$.80	$.20
3c Wheatland	$.80	$.20
3c Labor Day	$.80	$.20
3c Nassau Hall, Princeton	$.80	$.20
3c Devils Tower, Wyoming	$.60	$.20
3c Children & World Peace	$.45	$.20

1957	Unused	Used
3c Alexander Hamilton	$.40	$.20
3c Polio	$.40	$.20
3c Coast & Geodetic Survey	$.40	$.20
3c Architects	$.45	$.20
3c Steel Industry	$.40	$.20
3c International Naval Review	$.45	$.20
3c Oklahoma Statehood	$.45	$.20
3c School Teachers	$.55	$.20
4c 48-Star Flag	$.40	$.20
3c Shipbuilding	$.50	$.20
8c Ramon Magsaysay	$.40	$.20
3c Lafayette Bicentennial	$.50	$.20
3c Wildlife, Whooping Cranes	$.50	$.20
3c Religious Freedom	$.45	$.20
1958		
3c Gardening and Horticulture	$.45	$.20
3c Brussels Exhibition	$.45	$.20
3c James Monroe	$.45	$.20
3c Minnesota Statehood	$.40	$.20
3c International Geophysical Year	$.45	$.20

4c 48-Star Flag

*3c Wildlife,
Whooping
Cranes*

1958	Unused	Used
3c Gunston Hall, Virginia	$.40	$.20
3c Mackinac Bridge	$.45	$.20
4c Simon Bolivar	$.40	$.20
8c Bolivar	$.50	$.20
4c Atlantic Cable	$.45	$.20

1958-59 Lincoln Sesquicentennial		
1c Beardless Lincoln	$.40	$.20
3c Bust of Lincoln	$.60	$.20
4c Lincoln-Douglas Debates	$.70	$.20
4c Statue of Lincoln	$.50	$.20

1958		
4c Lajos Kossuth	$.40	$.20
8c Kossuth	$.50	$.20
4c Freedom of the Press	$.40	$.20
4c Overland Mail	$.50	$.20
4c Noah Webster	$.60	$.20
4c Forest Conservation	$.40	$.20
4c Fort Duquesne	$.60	$.20

4c Statue of Lincoln

4c Forest Conservation

1959	Unused	Used
4c Oregon Statehood	$.40	$.20
4c Jose de San Martin	$.40	$.20
8c San Martin	$.50	$.20
4c NATO	$.40	$.20
4c Arctic Exploration	$.60	$.20
8c World Peace/World Trade	$.50	$.20
4c Silver Centennial	$.60	$.20
4c St. Lawrence Seaway	$.60	$.20
4c 49-Star Flag	$.40	$.20
4c Soil Conservation	$.40	$.20
4c Petroleum Industry	$.70	$.20
4c Dental Health	$.60	$.20
4c Ernst Reuter	$.45	$.20
8c Reuter	$.50	$.20
4c Dr. Ephraim MacDowell	$.60	$.20
1960-61 American Credo Series		
4c George Washington	$.40	$.20
4c Benjamin Franklin	$.40	$.20
4c Thomas Jefferson	$.40	$.20
4c Francis Scott Key	$.60	$.20

1960-61 American Credo Series	Unused	Used
4c Abraham Lincoln	$.40	$.20
4c Patrick Henry	$.40	$.20
4c 50 Years of Boy Scouts	$.95	$.20
4c Winter Olympics	$.45	$.20
4c Thomas Masaryk	$.40	$.20
8c Masaryk	$.65	$.20
4c World Refugee Year	$.45	$.20
4c Water Conservation	$.40	$.20
4c SEATO	$.40	$.20
4c American Woman	$.40	$.20
4c 50-Star Flag	$.45	$.20
4c Pony Express	$1.10	$.20
4c Employ the Handicapped	$.40	$.20
4c World Forestry Congress	$.45	$.20
4c Mexican independence	$.45	$.20
1960		
4c U.S.-Japan Treaty	$.50	$.20
4c Ignacy Paderewski	$.40	$.20
8c Paderewski	$.60	$.20
4c Robert A. Taft	$.65	$.20

1960	Unused	Used
4c Boys' Clubs of America	$.60	$.20
4c 1st Automated Post Office	$1	$.20
4c Gustaf Mannerheim	$.40	$.20
8c Mannerheim	$.80	$.20
4c Camp Fire Girls	$1.25	$.20
4c Giuseppe Garibaldi	$.40	$.20
8c Garibaldi	$.60	$.20
4c Sen. Walter F. George	$1	$.20
4c Andrew Carnegie	$.80	$.20
4c John Foster Dulles	$.50	$.20
4c Echo I, Communications for Peace	$1	$.20

1961		
4c Mahatma Gandhi	$.40	$.20
8c Gandhi	$.60	$.20
4c Range Conservation	$.40	$.20
4c Horace Greeley	$1	$.20

1961-65 Civil War Centennial		
4c Fort Sumter	$.80	$.20
4c Battle of Shiloh	$.60	$.20

1961-65 Civil War Centennial	Unused	Used
5c Battle of Gettysburg	$1	$.20
5c Battle of the Wilderness	$.65	$.20
5c Appomattox	$1.20	$.20
1961		
4c Kansas Statehood	$.70	$.20
4c Sen. George W. Norris	$.60	$.20
4c Naval Aviation	$.60	$.20
4c Workmen's Compensation	$.40	$.20
4c Frederic Remington	$.60	$.20
4c Republic of China	$.65	$.20
4c Naismith, Basketball	$.85	$.20
4c Nursing	$.65	$.20

1962-1980

FAMOUS FIRSTS

Three significant events for philatelists occurred in 1962—the release of the Mystery Stamp, the release of a "do-over error," and the first Christmas stamp.

Postmasters at 305 United States post offices were curious about the sealed pouches they were issued but forbidden to open. Then, after astronaut John Glenn made the first U.S. trip into space and safely returned at 3:30 p.m., Feb. 20, 1962, the postmasters were allowed to open the packages. Inside were the Project Mercury stamps.

(See the "Christmas Stamps" and "Errors" chapters for more information about the first Christmas stamp and the "do-over" error.).

4c
Dag
Hammarskjold

1962	Unused	Used
4c New Mexico Statehood	$.40	$.20
4c Arizona Statehood	$.40	$.20
4c Project Mercury	$.40	$.20
4c Malaria Eradication	$.40	$.20
4c Charles Evans Hughes	$.40	$.20
4c Seattle World's Fair	$.40	$.20
4c Louisiana Statehood	$.60	$.20
4c Homestead Act	$.40	$.20
4c Girl Scouts	$.40	$.20
4c Sen. Brien McMahon	$.60	$.20
4c Apprenticeship	$.40	$.20
4c Sam Rayburn	$.60	$.20
4c Dag Hammerskjold	$.40	$.20
4c Dag Hammerskjold, yellow inverted	$.40	$.20
4c Christmas Wreath & Candles	$.40	$.20
4c Higher Education	$.40	$.20
4c Winslow Homer	$.50	$.20

1963-66		
5c Flag Over White House	$.20	$.20
1c Andrew Jackson, perforation 11 x 10-1/2	$.20	$.20

1963-66	Unused	Used
5c George Washington	$.35	$.20
1c Jackson, coil, perforation 10 vertically	$.20	$.20
5c Washington, coil	$1.50	$.20

1963		
5c Carolina Charter	$.60	$.20
5c Food for Peace	$.40	$.20
5c West Virginia Statehood	$.40	$.20
5c Emancipation Proclamation	$.45	$.20
5c Alliance for Progress	$.40	$.20
5c Cordell Hull	$.80	$.20
5c Eleanor Roosevelt	$.60	$.20
5c Science	$.40	$.20
5c City Mail Delivery	$.40	$.20
5c Red Cross Centenary	$.40	$.20
5c Christmas Tree & White House	$.80	$.20
5c John James Audubon	$.40	$.20

1964		
5c Sam Houston	$1.50	$.20
5c Charles M. Russell	$.50	$.20
5c New York World's Fair	$.60	$.20

1964	Unused	Used
5c John Muir	$.55	$.20
5c John F. Kennedy	$.95	$.20
5c New Jersey Tercentenary	$.85	$.20
5c Nevada Statehood	$.65	$.20
5c Register & Vote	$.40	$.20
5c William Shakespeare	$.40	$.20
5c Mayo Brothers	$.80	$.20
5c American Music	$.40	$.20
5c Homemakers	$.45	$.20
Christmas, block of 4	$3.95	$.50

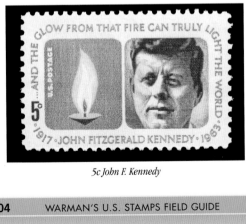

5c John F. Kennedy

1964	Unused	Used
5c Any single: Holly, Mistletoe, Poinsettia, Conifer Sprig	$1.25	$.20
5c Verrazano-Narrows Bridge	$.50	$.20
5c Fine Arts	$.40	$.20
5c Amateur Radio	$.80	$.20

1965		
5c Battle of New Orleans	$.70	$.20
5c Physical Fitness	$.40	$.20
5c Crusade Against Cancer	$.40	$.20
5c Winston Churchill	$.50	$.20
5c Magna Carta	$.45	$.20
5c International Cooperation Year	$.40	$.20
5c Salvation Army	$.40	$.20
5c Dante Alighieri	$.40	$.20
5c Herbert Hoover	$.50	$.20
5c Robert Fulton	$.40	$.20
5c Florida Settlement	$.50	$.20
5c Traffic Safety	$.40	$.20
5c John Singleton Copley	$.60	$.20

1965	Unused	Used
11c International Telecommunication Union	$.90	$.20
5c Adlai Stevenson	$.40	$.20
5c Christmas Angel	$.40	$.20
1965-81 Prominent Americans Series		
1c Thomas Jefferson, green	$.20	$.20
1-1/4c Albert Gallatin, light green	$.30	$.20
2c Frank Lloyd Wright, blue-gray	$.25	$.20
3c Francis Parkman, violet	$.30	$.20
4c Abraham Lincoln, black	$.35	$.20
1965-81 Prominent Americans Series		
5c George Washington, "unshaven," blue	$.35	$.20
5c Washington, "shaven," blue	$.35	$.20
6c Franklin D. Roosevelt, gray-brown	$.45	$.20
8c Albert Einstein, violet	$.60	$.20
10c Andrew Jackson, lilac	$.90	$.20
12c Henry Ford, black	$.60	$.20
13c John F. Kennedy, brown	$.90	$.25
15c Oliver Wendell Holmes, magenta, Type I: tie touches coat at bottom	$.75	$.20

1965-81 Prominent Americans Series	Unused	Used
15c Holmes, magenta, Type II: tie doesn't touch coat at bottom	$.75	$.20
15c Holmes, magenta, perforation 10	$.70	$.20
20c George C. Marshall, deep olive	$.95	$.20
25c Frederick Douglas, rose-lake	$1.10	$.20
30c John Dewey, red-lilac	$1.60	$.20
40c Thomas Paine, blue-black	$1.90	$.20
50c Lucy Stone, rose-magenta	$2.50	$.25
$1 Eugene O'Neill, dull purple	$4.25	$.20
$5 John Bassett Moore, gray-black	$18.50	$5.95

1966-81 Coils, Perforation 10 Horizontally		
3c Parkman	$.25	$.20
6c Roosevelt	$.50	$.20

5c Winston Churchill

25c Frederick Douglas, rose-lake

1966-81 Coils, Perforation 10 Vertically	Unused	Used
1c Jefferson	$.20	$.20
4c Lincoln	$.30	$.20
5c Washington, "unshaven"	$.35	$.20
5c Washington, "shaven"	$.35	$.20
6c Roosevelt	$.50	$.20
15c Holmes	$.65	$.20
$1 O'Neill	$5	$3
1966		
5c Migratory Bird Treaty	$.40	$.20
5c Humane Treatment of Animals	$.40	$.20
5c Indiana Statehood	$.80	$.20
5c American Circus	$.55	$.20
5c SIPEX	$.40	$.20
5c SIPEX souvenir sheet, imperforate	$.50	$.20
5c Bill of Rights	$.45	$.20
5c Polish Millennium	$.45	$.20
5c National Park Service	$.50	$.20
5c Marine Corps Reserve	$.45	$.20
5c Women's Clubs	$.45	$.20
5c Johnny Appleseed	$.70	$.20

1966	Unused	Used
5c Beautification of America	$.45	$.20
5c Great River Road	$.75	$.20
5c Savings Bonds	$.45	$.20
5c Christmas Madonna & Child	$.45	$.20
5c Mary Cassatt	$.45	$.20

1967		
5c National Grange	$.40	$.20
5c Canada Centenary	$.45	$.20
5c Erie Canal	$.45	$.20
5c Search for Peace	$.45	$.20
5c Henry David Thoreau	$.85	$.30
5c Nebraska Statehood	$.45	$.20
5c Voice of America		
5c Davy Crockett	$.60	$.20
Gemini Twins, pair	$4	$.55
5c Astronaut	$2.25	$.30
5c Capsule	$2.25	$.30
5c Urban Planning	$.40	$.20

5c American Circus

6c Support Our Youth

6c Father Marquette

Beautification of America, block of 4

6c Christmas, Nativity, precancelled

8c Yellowstone

1967	Unused	Used
5c Finnish Independence	$.40	$.20
5c Thomas Eakins	$.40	$.20
5c Christmas, Madonna & Child	$.40	$.20
5c Mississippi Statehood	$1	$.20
1968-71, Perforation 11		
6c Flag Over White House	$.40	$.20
Perforation 11 x 10-1/2		
6c Flag Over White House	$.40	$.20
8c Flag Over White House	$.50	$.20
Coils, Perforation 10 Vertically		
6c Flag Over White House	$.40	$.20
8c Flag Over White House	$.50	$.20
1968		
6c Illinois Statehood	$.90	$.20
6c Hemisfair '68	$.40	$.20
$1 Airlift	$4.95	$4
6c Support Our Youth	$.45	$.20
6c Law & Order	$.65	$.20
6c Register & Vote	$.60	$.20

1968	Unused	Used
Historic Flags, strip of 10	$10	$6
6c Fort Moultrie Flag	$1.90	$.75
6c Fort McHenry Flag	$1.90	$.65
6c Washington's Cruisers Flag	$1	$.65
6c Bennington Flag	$1	$.65
6c Rhode Island Flag	$1	$.65
6c 1st Stars & Stripes	$2.25	$.65
6c Bunker Hill Flag	$1	$.65
6c Grand Union Flag	$1.50	$.65
6c Philadelphia Light Horse Flag	$1	$.75
6c 1st Navy Jack	$1	$.65
6c Walt Disney	$1.75	$.40
6c Father Marquette	$1.20	$.20
6c Daniel Boone	$1.20	$.20
6c Arkansas River Navigation	$1.20	$.20
6c Leif Ericson	$.80	$.20
6c Cherokee Strip	$.60	$.20
6c John Trumbull	$1	$.20
6c Waterfowl Conservation	$.60	$.20

1968	Unused	Used
6c Christmas, Angel Gabriel	$.40	$.20
6c Chief Joseph	$.60	$.20
1969		
Beautification of America, block of 4	$6	$.70
6c Any single: Cities, Parks, Highways, Streets	$1.50	$.20
6c American Legion	$.40	$.20
6c Grandma Moses	$.40	$.20
6c Apollo 8, "Earthrise"	$.60	$.20
6c W.C. Handy	$.60	$.20
6c California Settlement	$.40	$.20
6c John Wesley Powell	$.50	$.20
6c Alabama Statehood	$.50	$.20
Botanical Congress, block of 4	$6	$.70
6c Any single: Douglas Fir, Lady's Slipper, Octotillo, Franklinia	$1.50	$.20
6c Daniel Webster, Dartmouth College Case	$.60	$.20
6c Professional Baseball	$1.95	$.20
6c Intercollegiate Football	$1	$.20
6c Dwight D. Eisenhower	$.50	$.20

1969	Unused	Used
6c Christmas, Winter Scene	$.40	$.20
6c Hope for the Crippled	$.40	$.20
6c William M. Harnett	$.40	$.20

1970		
Natural History, block of 4	$2.50	$.50
6c Any single: American Bald Eagle, African Elephant, Haida Ceremonial Canoe, Age of Reptiles	$.65	$.20
6c Maine Statehood	$.60	$.20
6c Wildlife Conservation, Buffalo	$.50	$.20

1970-74 Regular Issue, Perforation 11 x 10-1/2, 10-1/2 x 11, 11		
6c D.D. Eisenhower, dark blue-gray, dot before "USA"	$.45	$.20
7c Franklin, bright blue	$.45	$.20
8c Eisenhower, black, red and blue-gray, perforation 11, no dot before "USA"	$.45	$.20
8c Eisenhower, deep claret, from booklet, dot before "USA"	$.60	$.20
8c USPS Emblem, multicolored	$.45	$.20
14c Fiorello LaGuardia, gray-brown	$.95	$.20
16c Ernie Pyle, brown	$.95	$.20
6c Dr. Elizabeth Blackwell, violet	$.95	$.20

1970-74 Regular Issue, Perforation 11 x 10-1/2, 10-1/2 x 11, 11	Unused	Used
6c Amadeo P. Giannini, green	$.95	$.20
Coils, Perforation 10 Vertically		
6c Eisenhower, dark blue-gray	$.40	$.20
6c Eisenhower, deep claret	$.50	$.20
1970		
6c Edgar Lee Masters	$.50	$.20
6c Woman Suffrage	$.40	$.20
6c South Carolina	$.80	$.20
6c Stone Mountain Memorial	$.75	$.20
6c Fort Snelling	$.45	$.20
Anti-Pollution, block of 4	$3.50	$.70
6c Any single: Save Our Soil, Save Our Cities, Save Our Water, Save Our Air	$.90	$.20
6c Christmas, Nativity	$.40	$.20
Christmas secular, block of 4	$4.75	$.50
6c Any single: Locomotive, Toy Horse, Tricycle, Doll Carriage	$1.25	$.20
6c United Nations	$.40	$.20
6c Landing of the Pilgrims	$.40	$.20
Disabled Veterans and Servicemen pair	$.80	$.20

1970	Unused	Used
6c Disabled American Veterans	$.40	$.20
6c Honoring U.S. Servicemen	$.40	$.20

1971		
6c American Wool Industry	$.45	$.20
6c Gen. Douglas MacArthur	$.70	$.20
6c Blood Donors	$.40	$.20
8c Missouri Statehood	$.80	$.20
Wildlife Conservation, block of 4	$3	$.80
8c Any single: Trout, Alligator, Polar Bear, California Condor	$.70	$.20
8c Antarctic Treaty	$.45	$.20
8c American Revolution Bicentennial	$.50	$.20
8c John Sloane	$.65	$.20
Decade of Space Achievement, pair	$1	$.25
8c Lunar Module	$.50	$.20
8c Lunar Rover	$.50	$.20
8c Emily Dickinson	$.80	$.20
8c San Juan	$.45	$.20
8c Prevent Drug Abuse	$.60	$.20
8c CARE	$.40	$.20

1971	Unused	Used
Historic Preservation, block of 4	$3.50	$.75
8c Any single: Decatur House, Whaler Charles W. Morgan, Cable Car, San Xavier del Bac Mission	$.90	$.20
8c Christmas, Adoration of Shepherds	$.40	$.20
8c Christmas, Partridge	$.40	$.20

1972		
8c Sidney Lanier	$.80	$.20
8c Peace Corps	$.50	$.20

National Parks Centennial		
Cape Hattaras National Seashore, block of 4	$1	$.20
2c Any single: Ship's Hull, Lighthouse, Three Gulls, Two Gulls	$.25	$.20
6c Wolf Trap Farm	$.60	$.20
8c Yellowstone	$.50	$.20
8c Mt. McKinley	$.75	$.25
(An Airmail stamp is included in this issue.)		

1972		
8c Family Planning	$.50	$.20
Colonial American Craftsmen, block of 4	$2.75	$.75
8c Any single: Glass Blower, Silversmith, Wigmaker, Hatter	$.65	$.20

8c Mail Order Business

1972	Unused	Used
8c Olympics Bicycling	$.40	$.20
8c Olympics Bobsledding	$.40	$.20
15c Olympics Running	$.50	$.20
(An Airmail stamp is included in this issue.)		
8c Parent Teacher Association	$.50	$.20
Wildlife Conservation, block of 4	$1.95	$.75
8c Any single: Fur Seal, Cardinal, Brown Pelican, Bighorn Sheep	$.50	$.20
8c Mail Order Business	$.60	$.20

1972	Unused	Used
8c Osteopathic Medicine	$.80	$.20
8c Tom Sawyer	$1	$.20
8c Christmas, Angels	$.50	$.20
8c Christmas, Santa Claus	$.50	$.20
8c Pharmacy	$.75	$.20
8c Stamp Collecting	$.60	$.20
1973		
8c Love	$.40	$.20
Communication in Colonial Times		
8c Pamphlet Printing	$.55	$.20
8c Posting a Broadside	$.55	$.20
8c Post Rider	$.55	$.20
8c Drummer	$.55	$.20
Boston Tea Party, block of 4	$1.95	$.50
8c Any single: Merchant Vessel, Three Master, Boats and Hull, Boats and Pier	$.50	$.20
American Arts		
8c George Gershwin	$.40	$.20

1973	Unused	Used
8c Robinson Jeffers	$.40	$.20
8c Henry Ossawa Tanner	$.40	$.20
8c Willa Cather	$.50	$.20
8c Nicolaus Copernicus	$.40	$.20
Postal Service Employees, strip of 10	$4.95	$1.30
8c Stamp Counter	$.50	$.20
8c Mail Collection	$.50	$.20
8c Letters on Conveyor Belt	$.50	$.20
8c Parcels	$.50	$.50
8c Mail Canceling	$.50	$.20
8c Manual Letter Routing	$.50	$.20
8c Electronic Letter Routing	$.50	$.20
8c Loading Mail on Truck	$.50	$.20
8c Mail Carrier	$.50	$.20
8c Rural Mail Delivery	$.50	$.20
8c Harry S. Truman	$.60	$.20
6c Marconi's Spark Coil	$.40	$.20
8c Transistors and Circuit Board	$.40	$.20

1973	Unused	Used
15c Microphone, Speaker, TV Camera	$.75	$.50
(An Airmail stamp is included in this issue.)		
8c Lyndon B. Johnson	$.40	$.20
1973-74		
8c Angus & Longhorn Cattle	$.40	$.20
10c Chautauqua Tent	$.60	$.20
10c Wheat Fields, Train	$.55	$.20
8c Christmas, Madonna & Child	$.40	$.20
8c Christmas Tree in Needlepoint	$.40	$.20
1973-74 Regular Issue		
10c Crossed Flags	$.50	$.20
10c Jefferson Memorial	$.50	$.20
10c ZIP Code	$.50	$.20

FIRST DECIMAL, FIRST DIAMOND

Stamps had been issued in fractional values previously, but the 6.3-cent Liberty Bell stamp of 1974 was the first one issued in tenths of a cent. In subsequent years, decimal postage rates aimed primarily to serve bulk mailers became common. The first U.S. diamond-shaped stamps were the four Mineral Heritage issues in 1974.

Universal Postal Union Letter Writing, block of 8

Coils, Perforation 10 Vertically	Unused	Used
6.3c Liberty Bell, brick red	$.60	$.30
10c Crossed Flags	$.50	$.20
10c Jefferson Memorial	$.50	$.20
1974		
10c Veterans of Foreign Wars	$.50	$.20
10c Robert Frost	$.80	$.20
10c Expo '74 World's Fair	$.50	$.20
10c Horse Racing	$.90	$.20
10c Skylab	$.50	$.20
Universal Postal Union Letter Writing, block of 8	$5	$3.75
10c Any single stamp	$.65	$.30
Mineral Heritage, block of 4	$2.50	$.50
10c Any single: Petrified Wood, Tourmaline, Amethyst, Rhodocrasite	$.65	$.20
10c Kentucky Settlement	$.80	$.20
First Continental Congress, block of 4	$2.75	$.90
10c Any single: Carpenter's Hall, "We ask but for peace…," "Deriving their just powers…," Independence Hall	$.70	$.20
10c Energy Conservation	$.50	$.20

1974	Unused	Used
10c Legend of Sleepy Hollow	$.60	$.20
10c Retarded Children	$.60	$.20
10c Christmas Angel	$.50	$.20
10c Christmas, "The Road – Winter"	$.55	$.20
10c Christmas Dove Weather Vane, self-adhesive	$.55	$.45

1975		
10c Benjamin West	$.65	$.20
10c Paul Laurence Dunbar	$.55	$.20
10c D.W. Griffith	$.65	$.20
10c Pioneer 10	$.55	$.20
10c Mariner 10	$.55	$.20
10c Collective Bargaining	$.55	$.20
8c Sybil Ludington	$.50	$.20
10c Salem Poor	$.50	$.20
10c Haym Salomon	$.50	$.20
18c Peter Francisco	$.95	$.40
10c Battle of Lexington & Concord	$.60	$.20
10c Battle of Bunker Hill	$.60	$.20
Colonial Military Uniforms, block of 4	$2.50	$.60

1975	Unused	Used
10c Any single: Continental Army, Continental Navy, Continental Marines, American Militia	$.65	$.20
Apollo & Soyuz Space Cooperation, pair	1.10	$.20
10c Space Craft Linked	$.55	$.20
10c Space Craft Separated	$.55	$.20
10c International Women's Year	$.50	$.20
200 Years of Postal Service, block of 4	$2.75	$.50
10c Any single: Stagecoach & Trailer-Truck, Locomotives, Airplanes, Satellites	$.70	$.20
10c World Peace Through Law	$.60	$.20
Banking & Commerce pair	$1.35	$.20
10c Banking	$.70	$.20
10c Commerce	$.70	$.20
10c Christmas, Old Card	$.50	$.20
10c Christmas Madonna & Child	$.50	$.20

DESIGNED FOR DISPLAY

The definitive stamp series known as the Americana Issue was designed to be displayed in groups of four. This eighth Bureau issue featured a variety of iconic elements united somewhat by the color of the paper used and by phrases relating to the subjects that formed a border around each group of four.

As has become almost the norm, the set is replete with various anomalies–phosphorescent tagging varieties, paper varieties, perforation mistakes, color-omitted errors, and the first inverted image on a U.S. stamp in more than 50 years. These varieties are not listed here.

Declaration of Independence, souvenir sheet

1975-81 Americana Issue	Unused	Used
1c Inkwell & Quill, blue on greenish	$.20	$.20
2c Speaker's Stand, red-brown on greenish	$.20	$.20
3c Ballot Box, olive on greenish	$.20	$.20
4c Books, rose-magenta on cream	$.30	$.20
9c Capitol, slate green on white, perforation 11 x 10-1/2 (1977 booklet)	$1	$.75
9c Capitol, slate green, perforation 10 x 9-3/4 (1977 booklet)	$42.50	$20
9c Capitol, slate green on gray	$.45	$.20
10c Justice, violet on gray	$.45	$.20
11c Printing Press, orange on gray	$.60	$.20
12c Torch, red-brown on beige	$.60	$.20
13c Liberty Bell, brown (booklet)	$.90	$.20
13c Eagle & Shield, multicolored	$.50	$.20
15c Ft. McHenry Flag, multi, perforation 11	$.65	$.20
15c Flag, multi, perforation 11 x 10-1/2 (booklet)	$3.50	$.20
16c Statue of Liberty, blue, perforation 11 x 10-1/2	$1.20	$1.20
24c Old North Church, red on blue	$1.40	$.20
28c Ft. Nisqually, brown on blue	$1.95	$.25
29c Sandy hook Lighthouse, blue on light blue	$1.60	$1.55

$1 Rush Lamp, tan, brown, orange

1975-81 Americana Issue	Unused	Used
30c Schoolhouse, green on blue	$1.60	$.20
50c "Betty" Lamp, tan, black and orange	$2.60	$.25
$1 Rush Lamp, tan, brown, orange	$4.25	$.25
$2 Kerosene Lamp, tan, green, orange	$8.25	$1.10
$5 Railroad Lantern, tan, red-brown, orange	$20	$3
Coils, Perforation 10 Vertically		
3.1c Guitar, brown on yellow	$.50	$.50
7.7c Saxhorns, brown on yellow	$.70	$.70
7.9c Drum, carmine on yellow	$.70	$.70
8.4c Grand Piano, dark blue on yellow	$.70	$.70

Coils, Perforation 10 Vertically	Unused	Used
9c Capitol, slate green on gray	$.45	$.30
10c Justice, violet on gray	$.50	$.20
13c Liberty Bell, brown	$.65	$.20

1975-79 Coils, Perforation 10 Vertically		
15c Ft. McHenry Flag, multi	$.70	$.20
16c Statue of Liberty, ultramarine	$.90	$.90

1975-81 Regular Issue		
13c Flag & Independence Hall, blue & red, perforation 11 x 10-3/4	$.60	$.20
13c Flag & Hall, perforation 11-1/4	$.60	$.25
13c Flag & Capitol blue, red, perforation 11, (booklet)	$.70	$.70
Pair, with 9c Capitol	$2.95	$2.95
13c Flag & Capitol, perforation 10 x 9-3/4 (booklet)	$3.50	$3.50
Pair, with 9c Capitol	$42.50	---

Coil, Perforation 10 Vertically		
13c Flag over Independence Hall	$.65	$.20

Declaration of Independence, strip of 4

1976	Unused	Used
Spirit of '76, strip of 3	$2.10	$.50
13c Any single: Drummer Boy, Old Drummer, Fifer	$.70	$.20
13c Interphil	$.65	$.20
State Flags, pane of 50	$32.95	$28.95
13c Any single Flag	$.65	$.20
13c Telephone Centennial	$.65	$.20
13c Commercial Aviation	$.65	$.20
13c Chemistry	$.85	$.20
American Bicentennial, souvenir sheets	$40	$34.95

(Four reproductions of paintings of notable moments in the Revolution.)

1976	Unused	Used
13c Ben Franklin	$.65	$.20
Declaration of Independence, strip of 4	$6.95	$.70
13c Any single: Delegates standing, facing right, Delegates seated, facing right, Jefferson & Franklin standing, Hancock seated, facing left	$1.75	$.20
Olympics, block of 4	$4.25	$.95
13c Any single: Diving, Skiing, Running, Skating	$1.10	$.20
13c Clara Maass	$1.20	$.20
13c Adolph S. Ochs	$1.20	$.20
13c Christmas, Nativity	$.65	$.20
13c Christmas, "Winter Pastime"	$.65	$.20
1977		
13c Washington at Princeton	$.70	$.20
13c Sound Recording	$.70	$.20
Pueblo Pottery, block of 4	$3.75	$.95
13c Any single: Zia Pottery, San Ildefonso Pottery, Hopi Pottery, Acoma Pottery	$.95	$.20
13c Lindbergh Flight	$.65	$.20
13c Colorado Statehood	$.65	$.20
Butterflies, block of 4	$2.75	$.70
13c Any single: Swallowtail, Checkerspot, Dogface, Orange-tip	$.70	$.20

1977	Unused	Used
13c Marquis de Lafayette	$1	$.20
Skilled Hands for Independence, block of 4	$3.50	$.70
13c Any single: Seamstress, Blacksmith, Wheelwright, Leatherworker	$.90	$.20
13c Peace Bridge	$.70	$.20
13c Battle of Oriskany	$.65	$.20
Energy, pair	$1.50	$.30
13c Conservation	$.75	$.20
13c Development	$.75	$.20
13c Alta, Calif., First Settlement	$.65	$.20
13c Articles of Confederation	$1	$.20
13c Talking Pictures	$.70	$.20
13c Surrender at Saratoga	$.70	$.20
13c Christmas, Washington Praying	$.65	$.20
13c Christmas, Mailbox	$.65	$.20

1978		
13c Carl Sandburg	$.80	$.20
Capt. James Cook, pair	$2	$.25
13c Portrait/Alaska	$.65	$.20
13c Ship/Hawaii	$.65	$.20

1978-80 Regular Issues	Unused	Used
13c Indian Head Penny	$.65	$.20
(15c) "A" & Eagle, orange, perforation 11	$.65	$.20
(15c) "A" & Eagle, orange, perforation 11 x 10-1/2 (booklet)	$.65	$.20
15c Roses, multi, perforation 10 (booklet)	$.95	$.20
Windmill booklet, strip of 5	$5	$.50
15c Any single: Virginia, Rhode Island, Massachusetts, Illinois, Texas	$1	$.20
Coil, Perforation 10 Vertically		
(15c) "A" & Eagle, orange	$.65	$.20
1978		
15c Harriett Tubman	$1.25	$.20
Folk Art Basket Design Quilts, block of 4	$3.50	$1
15c Any single: Orange-Flowered, Red and White Stars, Orange Striped, Black Plaid	$.90	$.20
American Dance, block of 4	$3.95	$1
13c Any single: Ballet, Dance in Theater, Folk Dance, Modern Dance	$1	$.20
13c French Alliance	$.75	$.20
13c Early Cancer Detection	$1.50	$.20
13c Jimmie Rogers	$.90	$.20

1978	Unused	Used
15c George M. Cohan	$1	$.20
CAPEX souvenir sheet of 8	$4.50	$4.50
CAPEX, block of 8	$5	---
13c Any single: Cardinal, Mallard, Canada Goose, Blue Jay, Moose, Chipmunk, Red Fox, Raccoon	$.65	$.65
15c Photography	$.75	$.20
15c Viking Missions to Mars	$.75	$.20
American Owls, block of 4	$3.95	$1
15c Any single: Great Gray Owl, Saw-whet Owl, Barred Owl, Great Horned Owl	$1	$.20
American Trees, block of 4	$4.25	$.70
15c Any single: Giant Sequoia, White Pine, White Oak, Gray Birch	$1.10	$.20
15c Christmas, Madonna & Child	$.75	$.20
15c Christmas, Hobby Horse	$.75	$.20

1979		
15c Robert F. Kennedy	$1	$.20
15c Dr. Martin Luther King Jr.	$1.20	$.20
15c International Year of the Child	$.75	$.20
15c John Steinbeck	$.75	$.20

1979	Unused	Used
15c Albert Einstein	$1.20	$.20
American Folk Art Toleware, block of 4	$3.95	$.70
15c Any single: Straight-Spouted Coffee Pot, Tea Caddy, Sugar Bowl, Curved-Spouted Coffee Pot	$1	$.20
American Architecture, block of 4	$4.95	$.70
15c Any single: Virginia Rotunda, Baltimore Cathedral, Boston State House, Philadelphia Exchange	$1.25	$.20
Endangered Flora, block of 4	$3.95	$.75
15c Any single: Persistent Trillium, Hawaiian Wild Broadbean, Contra Costa Wallflower, Antioch Dunes Evening Primrose	$1	$.20
15c Seeing Eye Dogs	$.75	$.20
15c Special Olympics	$.75	$.20
15c John Paul Jones, perforation 11 x 12	$.95	$.25
15c John Paul Jones, perforation 11	$.80	$.50
15c John Paul Jones, perforation 12	$2,500	---
10c Olympics Javelin	$.80	$.20
Summer Olympic Games, block of 4	$3.95	$.75
15c Any single: Running, Women's Swimming, Rowing, Equestrian	$1	$.20
Winter Olympics, perforation 11-1/4 x 10-1/2, block of 4	$4.50	$.95

1979	Unused	Used
15c Any single: Speed Skating, Downhill Skiing, Ski Jumping, Ice Hockey	$1.15	$.20
Winter Olympic Games, perforation 11, block of 4	$12.50	$3.50
15c Any single: Speed Skating, Downhill Skiing, Ski Jumping, Ice Hockey	$3	$.60
15c Christmas, Virgin & Child	$.75	$.20
15c Christmas, Santa Claus	$.75	$.20
15c Will Rogers	$.75	$.20
15c Vietnam Veterans	$1	$.20

1980		
15c W.C. Fields	$.75	$.20
15c Benjamin Banneker	$1	$.20
National Letter Writing Week, strip of 6	$6	---
15c Any single: Letters Preserve Memories, P.S. Write Soon (purple, green, or red), Letters Lift Spirits, Letters Shape Opinions	$1	$.20

1980-81 Americana Coils, Perforation 10 Vertically		
1c Inkwell & Quill	$.20	$.20
3.5c Violins	$.40	$.40
12c Torch	$.60	$.60

1981 Regular Issue	Unused	Used
(18c) "B" & Eagle, violet	$.80	$.20

1981 Regular Issue		
(18c) "B" & Eagle, violet, perforation 10 (booklet)	$1	$.20

Coil, Perf 10 Vertically		
(18c) "B" & Eagle, violet	$.90	$.20

1980		
15c Frances Perkins	$.70	$.20
15c Dolley Madison	$.70	$.20
15c Emily Bissell	$1	$.20
15c Helen Keller & Anne Sullivan	$1	$.20
15c Veterans Administration	$.75	$.20
15c Bernardo de Galvez	$.90	$.20
Coral Reefs, block of 4	$3.50	$.75
15c Any single: Brain Coral, Elkhorn Coral, Chalice Coral, Finger Coral	$.90	$.20
15c Organized labor	$.80	$.20
15c Edith Wharton	$.75	$.20
15c Education	$.75	$.20

Heiltsuk, Bella Bella
Indian Art USA 15c

Chilkat Tlingit
Indian Art USA 15c

Tlingit
Indian Art USA 15c

Bella Coola
Indian Art USA 15c

American Folk Art Indian Masks, block of 4

(18c) "B" & Eagle, violet

15c Education

1980	Unused	Used
American Folk Art Indian Masks, block of 4	$5.50	$.75
15c Any single: Bella Bella, Chilkat Tlingit, Tlingit, Bella Coola	$1.40	$.20
American Architecture, block of 4	$5.50	$.75
15c Any single: Smithsonian Institution, Trinity Church, Penn Academy, Lyndhurst	$1.25	$.20
15c Christmas, Madonna & Child Window	$.75	$.20
15c Christmas Wreath & Toys	$.75	$.20

1980-1988

DUELING DEFINITIVES

Two handsome regular-issue-stamps series ran concurrently for two decades at the end of the 20th century.

The Great Americans series became a portrait gallery of sketches of 63 individuals. In a notable departure from previous definitive issues, these included only two United States presidents, Thomas Jefferson and Harry S. Truman. Rather, the series remarkably honored men and women from every American era and from many walks of life.

Twenty-three artists prepared the portraits, and four printing firms were used in the series, which ran from 1980-99.

For much of that time, 1981-95, a series known as the Transportation Coils also was available. After a rather staid beginning with such subjects as a Locomotive, Stagecoach, and Sleigh, the series offered such whimsical subjects as an Elevator, Lunch Wagon and Popcorn Wagon.

In later installments of the series and the introduction of the subsequent Flora and Fauna Series, the "cents" signs were removed from the denominations to allow artists more freedom in designs. With the introduction of dollar values, however, confusion emerged: Did the "1" on the Omnibus stamp represent a cent or a dollar? So dollar signs were used for the higher denominations

From early days of postage stamps, printers had included the printing plate numbers in the selvage of the sheets of stamps. Starting with the Flag and Anthem issue, printers also added tiny plate numbers in the lower margins of some stamps in coil rolls. Collecting these varieties, some of which are scarce, has become a popular specialty. These and other varieties of paper, ink, gum and perforation on these series are not listed here.

2c Igor Stravinsky, brown-black   *3c Henry Clay, olive-green*

1980-85 Great Americans Issue	Unused	Used
1c Dorothea Dix, black	$.20	$.20
2c Igor Stravinsky, brown-black	$.20	$.20
3c Henry Clay, olive-green	$.20	$.20
4c Carl Schurz, violet	$.20	$.20
5c Pearl S. Buck, henna brown	$.50	$.20
6c Walter Lippmann, orange-vermilion	$.30	$.30
7c Abraham Baldwin, bright carmine	$.75	$.35
8c Henry Knox, olive-black	$.50	$.45
9c Sylvanus Thayer, dark green	$.45	$.45
10c Richard Russell, Prussian blue	$1	$.40
11c Alden Partridge, dark blue	$.60	$.25
13c Crazy Horse, light maroon	$.65	$.20
14c Sinclair Lewis, slate green	$.90	$.20
17c Rachel Carson, green	$.75	$.20
18c George Mason, dark blue	$.90	$.20
19c Sequoyah, brown	$.85	$.50
20c Ralph Bunche, claret	$1	$.20
20c Thomas H. Gallaudet, green	$1.50	$.20
20c Harry S. Truman, black	$.90	$.20
22c John James Audubon, dark chalky blue	$1.25	$.20

4c Carl Schurz,
violet

5c Pearl S. Buck,
henna brown

6c Walter Lippmann,
orange-vermilion

8c Henry Knox,
olive-black

11c Alden Partridge,
dark blue

14c Sinclair Lewis,
slate green

17c Rachel Carson,
green

18c George Mason,
dark blue

*19c Sequoyah,
brown*

*20c Harry S. Truman,
black*

15c Everett Dirksen

15c Whitney M. Young

1980-85 Great Americans Issue	Unused	Used
30c Frank C. Laubach, olive-gray	$1.50	$.20
35c Dr. Charles R. Drew, gray	$1.55	$.50
37c Robert Milikan, blue	$1.60	$.20
39c Grenville Clark, rose-lilac	$1.60	$.20
40c Lillian M. Gilbreth, dark green	$1.60	$.20
50c Chester W. Nimitz, brown	$1.95	$.20
1981		
15c Everett Dirksen	$.80	$.20
15c Whitney M. Young	$1	$.20
Flowers, block of 4	$4.50	---
18c Any single: Rose, Camelia, Dahlia, and Lily	$1.15	$.20
American Wildlife, booklet of 10	$12	---
Any single: 18c Bighorn, Puma, Harbor Seal, American Buffalo, Brown Bear, Polar Bear, Elk, Moose, Whitetail Deer, Pronghorn	$1.20	$.20
1981 Flag & Anthem Issue		
18c "…for amber waves of grain"	$.85	$.20
18c "from sea to shining sea"	$.85	$.20
6c Circle of Stars	$3	$3

Flowers, block of 4

American Wildlife, booklet of 10

18c "...for amber waves of grain"

18c "from sea to shining sea"

18c Professional Management

1981 Flag & Anthem Issue	Unused	Used
18c "purple mountain majesties"	$.85	$.20
Pair, 6c and 18c	$4	$3.50
20c Flag Over Supreme Court	$.95	$.20
20c Flag Over Supreme Court, coil	$.95	$.20
20c Flag Over Supreme Court, booklet	$.95	$.20
1981-84		
1c Omnibus, violet	$.20	$.20
2c Locomotive, black	$.20	$.20
3c Hand Car, dark green	$.20	$.20
4c Stagecoach, reddish-brown	$.20	$.20
5c Motorcycle, gray-green	$.25	$.20
5.2c Sleigh, carmine	$.70	$.20
5.9c Bicycle, blue	$.70	$.70
7.4c Baby Buggy, brown	$.75	$.70
9.3c Mail Wagon, carmine-rose	$1	$.25
10.9c Hansom Cab, purple	$1	$.50
11c Caboose, red	$.75	$.25
17c Electric Auto, ultramarine	$.75	$.20
18c Surrey, dark brown	$.85	$.20
20c Fire Pumper, vermilion	$.95	$.20

20c Flag Over Supreme Court

18c American Red Cross

18c Savings & Loans

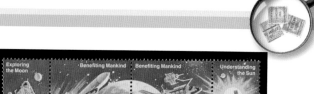

Space Achievement, block of 8

$9.35 Eagle & Full Moon, booklet

18c Edna St. Vincent Millay

Preservation of Wildlife Habitats, block of 4

1981-84	Unused	Used
$9.35 Eagle & Full Moon, booklet	$42.50	$37.50
18c American Red Cross	$.90	$.20
18c Savings & Loans	$.90	$.20
Space Achievement, block of 8	$7.95	---
18c Any individual stamp	$1	$.30
18c Professional Management	$.90	$.20
Preservation of Wildlife Habitats, block of 4	$4.95	---

1981	Unused	Used
18c Any single: Great Blue Heron, Badger, Grizzly Bear, and Ruffed Grouse	$1.25	$.20
18c International Year of the Disabled	$1	$.20
18c Edna St. Vincent Millay	$1	$.20
18c Alcoholism	$1.50	$.20
American Architecture, block of 4	$6	---
18c Any single: New York University Library, Biltmore Home, Palace of the Arts, National	$1.50	$.20
18c Babe Zaharias	$1	$.50
18c Bobby Jones	$1.95	$.35
18c Frederic Remington	$.90	$.20
18c James Hoban	$1	$1
20c James Hoban	$1	$.20
Battle of Yorktown & Virginia Capes, pair	$2.75	---
18c Yorktown	$1.40	$.70
18c Virginia Capes	$1.40	$.70
(20c) Christmas, Madonna & Child	$.95	$.20
(20c) Christmas, Bear on Sleigh	$.95	$.20
20c John Hanson	$1.20	$.20
Desert Plants, block of 4	$4.95	---

18c International Year of the Disabled

18c Alcoholism

American Architecture, block of 4

18c Babe Zaharias

18c James Hoban, Ireland

18c James Hoban, U.S.

20c James Hoban, U.S.

Battle of Yorktown & Virginia Capes, pair

Desert Plants, block of 4

1981	Unused	Used
20c Any single: Barrel Cactus, Saguaro Cactus, Agave, and Beavertail Cactus	$1.25	.$20
(20c) "C" & Eagle, brown	$.90	$.20
(20c) "C" & Eagle, brown, coil	$1	$.20
(20c) "C" & Eagle, brown, booklet (small)	$.95	$.20
20c Bighorn, booklet	$.95	$.20

1982		
20c Franklin D. Roosevelt	$1.20	$.20
20c Love	$1	$.20
20c George Washington	$1	$.20
State Birds & Flowers Issue, pane of 50	$55	---
20c Any single stamp	$1	$.55
20c U.S.-Netherlands	$1	$.20
20c Library of Congress	$1.40	$.20
20c Consumer Education, sky blue, coil	$1.10	$.20
Knoxville World's Fair, block of 4	$7	---
20c Any single, coil: Solar Energy, Synthetic Fuels, Breeder Reactor, Fossil Fuels	$1.75	$.20
20c Horatio Alger	$1.35	$.20
20c Aging Together	$1	$.20
20c The Barrymores	$1	$.20

(20c) "C" & Eagle, brown

(20c) "C" & Eagle, brown, coil

20c Bigborn, booklet

20c Franklin D. Roosevelt

20c Love

1982	Unused	Used
20c Dr. Mary Walker	$1.10	$.20
20c International Peace Garden	$1.10	$.20
20c American Libraries	$1.10	$.20
20c Jackie Robinson	$2.95	$.20

20c U.S.-Netherlands

20c George Washington

20c Library of Congress

1982	Unused	Used
20c Touro Synagogue	$1.10	$.20
20c Wolf Trap Farm	$1.10	$.20
American Architecture, block of 4	$6.75	---
20c Any single: Falling Water, Illinois Institute of Technology, Gropius House, Dulles Airport	$1.70	$.20
20c Francis of Assisi	$1.10	$.20
20c Ponce de Leon	$1.10	$.20

20c Consumer Education, sky blue

20c Horatio Alger

Knoxville World's Fair, block of 4

20c Aging Together

20c The Barrymores

20c Dr. Mary Walker

20c International Peace Garden

20c Jackie Robinson

20c American Libraries

20c Touro Synagogue

20c Wolf Trap Farm

American Architecture, block of 4

1982	Unused	Used
13c Christmas, Kitten & Puppy	$1	$.20
20c Christmas, Madonna & Child	$1	$.20
Christmas, Winter Fun, block of 4	$6.25	---
20c Any single: Sledding, Snow Man, Skating, Tree Trimming	$1.60	$.20

1983		
20c Science & Industry	$1	$.20
Balloons, block of 4	$4.95	---
20c Any single: Intrepid, Explorer, Hot Air, heading left, Hot Air, heading right	$1.25	$.20
20c U.S.-Sweden	$1	$.20
20c Civilian Conservation Corps	$1	$.20
20c Joseph Priestley	$1	$.20
20c Voluntarism	$1	$.20
20c U.S.-Germany	$1	$.20
20c Brooklyn Bridge	$1.25	$.20
20c Norris Hydroelectric Dam	$1.10	$.20
20c Physical Fitness	$1.10	$.20
20c Scott Joplin	$1.25	$.20

20c Francis of Assisi

20c Ponce de Leon

20c Christmas, Madonna & Child

13c Christmas, Kitten & Puppy

Christmas, Winter Fun, block of 4

20c Science & Industry

20c U.S.-Sweden

20c Civilian Conservation Corps

Balloons, block of 4

20c Voluntarism

20c Joseph Priestley

20c U.S.-Germany

20c Brooklyn Bridge

20c Norris Hydroelectric Dam

1983	Unused	Used
20c Medal of Honor	$1.25	$.20
20c Babe Ruth	$1.95	$.25
20c Nathaniel Hawthorne	$1.25	$.20
Summer Olympics, block of 4	$6	---
20c Any single: Discus, High Jump, Archery, Boxing	$1.50	$1
20c Treaty of Paris	$1.25	$.20
20 Civil Service	$1.10	$.20
20c Metropolitan opera	$1	$.20
American Inventors, block of 4	$7.50	---
20c Any single: Charles Steinmetz, Edwin Armstrong, Nikola Tesla, Philo T. Farnsworth	$1.90	$.20
Streetcars, block of 4	$7.95	---
20c Any single: First Streetcar, Early Electric, "Bob Tail" Horse Car, St. Charles Streetcar	$2	$.20
20c Christmas, Madonna & Child	$1.10	$.20
20c Christmas, Santa Claus	$1.10	$.20
20c Martin Luther	$1.30	$.20
1984		
20c Alaska Statehood	$1.30	$.20
Winter Olympics, block of 4	$5.25	---

20c Physical Fitness

20c Medal of Honor

20c Scott Joplin

20c Babe Ruth

20c Nathaniel
Hawthorne

1984	Unused	Used
20c Any single: Ice Dancing, Downhill Skiing, Cross-Country Skiing, Hockey	$1.35	$.20
20c Federal Deposit Insurance Corp.	$1	$.20
20c Love	$1	$.20

1984	Unused	Used
20c Carter G. Woodson	$1	$.20
20c Soil & Water Conservation	$1	$.20
20c Credit Union Act	$1	$.20
Orchids, block of 4	$5.95	---
20c Any single: Wild Pink, Yellow Lady's Slipper, Spreading Pogonia, Pacific Calypso	$1.50	$.25
20c Hawaii Statehood	$1.25	$.20
20c National Archives	$1	$.20
Summer Olympics, block of 4	$6.50	---
20c Any single: Diving, Long Jump, Wrestling, Kayak	$1.55	$.25
20c Louisiana World Expo	$1.50	$.20
20c Health Research	$1	$.20
20c Douglas Fairbanks	$2	$.20
20c Jim Thorpe	$1.50	$.20
20c John McCormack	$1.25	$.20
20c St. Lawrence Seaway	$1	$.20
20c Waterfowl Preservation Act	$1.25	$.20
20c Roanoke Voyages	$1.10	$.20
20c Herman Melville	$1.10	$.20
20c Horace Moses	$1.50	$.20

Summer Olympics, block of 4

20c Treaty of Paris

*20c
Civil
Service*

American Inventors, block of 4

20c Christmas, Santa Claus

*20c Christmas,
Madonna & Child*

20c Martin Luther

20c Federal Deposit Insurance
Corp.

20c Credit Union Act

20c Soil & Water Conservation

1984	Unused	Used
20c Smokey Bear	$1.25	$.20
20c Roberto Clemente	$1.50	$.65
Dogs, block of 4	$6.95	---
20c Any single: Beagle, Boston Terrier; Chesapeake Bay Retriever, Cocker Spaniel; Alaskan Malamute, Collie; Black & Tan Coonhound, American Foxhound	$1.75	$.20
20c Crime Prevention	$1	$.20
20c Hispanic Americans	$1.10	$.20
20c Family Unity	$1.75	$.20
20c Eleanor Roosevelt	$1.10	$.20
20c A Nation of Readers	$1.50	$.20
20c Christmas, Madonna & Child	$1	$.20
20c Christmas, Santa Claus	$1.25	$.20
20c Vietnam Veterans Memorial	$2	$.20
1985		
20c Jerome Kern	$1	$.20
1985 Regular Issue		
(22c) "D" & Eagle, green	$1.10	$.20
(22c) "D" & Eagle, green, coil	$1.10	$.20
(22c) "D" & Eagle, green, booklet (small)	$2.75	$.20

20c National Archives

20c Alaska Statehood

20c Love

20c Carter G. Woodson

1985 Regular Issue	Unused	Used
22c Flag Over Capitol	$1.10	$.20
22c Flag Over Capitol, coil	$1.10	$.20
22c Flag Over Capitol Landscape, booklet	$1.50	$.20
Seashells booklet, strip of 5	$5.50	---
22c Any single: Frilled Dogwinkle, Reticulated Helmet, New England Neptune, Calico Scallop, Lightning Whelk	$1.10	$.20
$10.75 Eagle & Half Moon	$39.95	$19.95
1985-87 Transportation Coils		
3.4c School Bus, dark bluish-green	$.50	$.50
4.9c Buckboard, brown-black	$.50	$.50
5.5c Star Route Truck, deep magenta	$.60	$.60
6c Tricycle, red-brown	$.50	$.50
7.1c Tractor, lake	$.60	$.60
8.3c Ambulance, green	$.60	$.60
8.5c Tow Truck, dark Prussian green	$.60	$.40
10.1c Oil Wagon, slate blue	$.70	$.50
11c Stutz Bearcat, dark green	$.70	$.70
12c Stanley Steamer, dark blue	$.70	$.65
12.5c Push Cart, olive-green	$.70	$.40

20c Hawaii Statehood

20c Louisiana World Expo

Summer Olympics, block of 4

*20c
Douglas
Fairbanks*

20c Health Research

*20c John
McCormack,
Ireland*

*20c John
McCormack,
U.S.*

20c St. Lawrence Seaway

20c Waterfowl Preservation Act

*20c
Roanoke
Voyages*

*20c Herman
Melville*

*20c
Smokey
Bear*

*20c Roberto
Clemente*

*Dogs,
block of 4*

1985-87 Transportation Coils	Unused	Used
14c Ice Boat, sky blue	$.70	$.70
17c Dog Sled, sky blue	$1.10	$.30
25c Bread Wagon, orange-brown	$1.20	$.20

1985		
22c Mary McLeod Bethune	$1.35	$.20
American Folk Art, Duck Decoys, block of 4	$7.95	---
22c Any single: Broadbill, Mallard, Canvasback, Redhead	$2	$.20
22c Winter Special Olympics	$1.25	$.20
22c Love	$1.25	$.20
22c Rural Electrification Administration	$1.50	$.20
22c Ameripex '86	$1.25	$.20
22c Abigail Adams	$1.25	$.20
22c Frederic Auguste Bartholdi	$1	$.20
18c George Washington & Monument, multi, coil	$1	$.20
21.1c Sealed Envelopes, multi, coil	$1.25	$1.20
22c Korean War Veterans	$1.25	$.20
22c Social Security Act	$1.25	$.20
22c World War I Veterans	$1.50	$.20

20c Crime Prevention

20c Family Unity

20c Hispanic Americans

20c Eleanor Roosevelt

20c A Nation of
Readers

20c Christmas,
Madonna & Child

20c Christmas,
Santa Claus

20c Vietnam Veterans Memorial

20c Jerome Kern

(22c) "D" & Eagle, green

(22c) "D" & Eagle, green, booklet

22c Flag Over Capitol

1985	Unused	Used
Horses, block of 4	$15.95	---
22c Any single: Quarter Horse, Morgan, Saddlebred, and Appaloosa	$4	$.40
22c Public Education	$2.25	$.20
International Youth Year, block of 4	$9.95	---
22c Any single: YMCA Youth Camping, Boy Scouts, Big Brothers/Big Sisters, Camp Fire	$2.50	$.20
22c Help End Hunger	$1.25	$.20
22c Christmas, Genoa Madonna	$1	$.20
22c Christmas, Poinsettia	$1	$.20

1986		
22c Arkansas Statehood	$1	$.20

1986-94 Great Americans Regular Issue		
1c Margaret Mitchell, brownish-vermilion	$.20	$.20
2c Mary Lyon, bright blue	$.25	$.20
3c Dr. Paul Dudley White, bright blue	$.35	$.20
4c Father Edward Flanagan, blue-violet	$.25	$.20
5c Hugo L. Black, dark olive-green	$.60	$.20
5c Luis Munoz Marin, carmine	$.35	$.20
10c Red Cloud, lake	$.50	$.20
14c Julia Ward Howe, crimson	$1.25	$.50

22c Flag Over Capitol, coil

*22c Mary
McLeod Bethune*

*22c Winter
Special
Olympics*

*Seashells booklet,
strip of 5*

22c Love

22c Rural Electrification Administration

22c Ameripex '86

22c Abigail Adams

22c Frederic Auguste Bartholdi

18c George Washington & Monument, multi

21.1c Sealed Envelopes, coil

22c Korean War Veterans

22c World War I Veterans

Horses, block of 4

22c Christmas,
Poinsettia

22c Public
Education

22c Christmas,
Genoa Madonna

International Youth Year, block of 4

5c Hugo
L. Black,
*dark
olive-
green*

22c Arkansas Statehood

*5c Luis Munoz Marin,
carmine*

*10c Red Cloud,
lake*

*14c Julia Ward Howe,
crimson*

*1c Margaret Mitchell,
brownish-vermilion*

*2c Mary Lyon,
bright blue*

*3c Dr. Paul Dudley
White, bright blue*

1986-94 Great Americans Regular Issue	Unused	Used
15c Buffalo Bill Cody, claret	$.80	$.20
17c Belva Ann Lockwood, dull blue-green	$.85	$.20
20c Dr. Virginia Apgar, red-brown	$.85	$.30
21c Chester Carlson, blue-violet	$1	$.75
23c Mary Cassatt, purple	$1	$.20
25c Jack London, blue	$1.10	$.20
28c Sitting Bull, myrtle green	$1.30	$1
29c Earl Warren, blue	$1.30	$.90
29c Thomas Jefferson, indigo	$1.30	$.20
35c Dennis Chavez, black	$1.40	$1.20
40c Claire Chennault, dark blue	$1.60	$.25
45c Dr. Harvey Cushing, bright blue	$1.80	$.20
52c Hubert H. Humphrey, purple	$2	$.20
56c John Harvard, scarlet	$3.25	$3.25
65c H.H. "Hap" Arnold, dark blue	$3	$3
75c Wendell Willkie, deep magenta	3.50	$.50
$1 Bernard Revel, dark Prussian green	$4	$.40
$1 Johns Hopkins, deep blue	$5	$.20
$2 William Jennings Bryan, bright violet	$8	$7.50

1986-94 Great Americans Regular Issue	Unused	Used
$5 Bret Harte, copper-red	$19.50	$3.25
25c London, blue (booklet)	$1.10	$.20

1986		
Stamp Collecting booklet, pane of 4	$4.25	---
22c Any single: Circular Hand stamp, Boy and Album, Magnifying Glass, First-Day Canceller	$1.10	$.50
22c Love	$1	$.20
22c Sojourner Truth	$1.25	$.20
22c Republic of Texas	$1.75	$.20
Fish booklet, pane of 5	$15.95	---
22c Any single: Muskellunge, Atlantic Cod, Largemouth Bass, luefin Tuna, Catfish	$3.20	$.20
22c Public Hospitals	$1	$.20
22c Duke Ellington	$1	$.20
Ameripex '86 Sheetlets of Presidents, set of 4	$43	---
22c Any single stamp	$1.25	$1
Arctic Explorers, block of 4	$8.25	---
22c Any single: Elisha Kent Kane, Adolphus W. Greely, Vihjalmur Stefansson, Robert E. Peary & Matthew Henson	$2.10	$.65
22c Statue of Liberty	$1	$.20

1986-87 Transportation Coil Issues Redesigned	Unused	Used
1c Omnibus, violet ("1 USA")	$.20	$.20
2c Locomotive, black ("2 USA")	$.20	$.20
4c Stagecoach, reddish-brown (legend is 1.75 mm shorter than on 1981 series)	$.25	$.25
8.3c Ambulance, green (legend is .5 mm shorter than on 1985 series)	$.20	$.20

1986		
American Folk Art Navajo Blankets, block of 4	$12.95	---
22c Any single: Stripes & Diamonds, 2 Diamonds, 5 Diamonds, 4 Diamonds	$3.25	$.20
22c T. S. Eliot	$1	$.25
American Folk Art Carved Figures, block of 4	$4.95	---
22c Any single: Highlander Figure, Ship Figurehead, Nautical Figure and Cigar Store Figure	$1.25	$.20
22c Christmas, Madonna	$1	$.20
22c Christmas, Village Scene	$1	$.20

1987		
22c Michigan Statehood	$1.10	$.20

*4c Father Edward
Flanagan, blue-violet*

*17c Belva Ann Lockwood,
dull blue-green*

*21c Chester Carlson,
blue-violet*

23c Mary Cassatt, purple

25c Jack London, blue

Stamp Collecting booklet, pane of 4

1987	Unused	Used
22c Pan American Games	$1.25	$.20
22c Love	$1.25	$.20
22c Jean Baptiste du Sable	$1.25	$.20
22c Enrico Caruso	$1.25	$.20
22c Girl Scouts	$1.25	$.20
1987-88 Transportation Coils		
3c Conestoga Wagon, claret	$.25	$.20
5c Milk Wagon, black	$.40	$.25
5.3c Elevator, black	$.50	$.50
7.6c Carretta, brown	$.70	$.20
8.4c Wheelchair, deep claret	$.80	$.30
10c Canal Boat, blue	$.50	$.20
13c Patrol Wagon, black	$1.10	$1
13.2c Coal Car, slate green	$.70	$.20
15c Tugboat, violet	$.70	$.20
16.7c Popcorn Wagon, rose	$.80	$.20
17.5c Racing Car, dark violet	$1	$1

1987-88 Transportation Coils	Unused	Used
20c Cable Car, blue-violet	$1	$.20
20.5c Fire Engine, rose	$1	$.50
21c Railroad Mail Car, olive-green	$1	$.30
24.1c Tandem Bicycle, deep ultramarine	$1.40	$1.30

1987		
Special Occasions, booklet pane of 10 (eight designs)	$29	---
22c Congratulations!	$2.50	$.45
22c Get Well!	$3.50	$.45
22c Thank You!	$3.50	$.75
22c Love You, Dad!	$3	$.45
22c Best Wishes!	$3	$.75
22c Happy Birthday!	$2.50	$.65
22c Love You, Mother!	$4	$.75
22c Keep in Touch!	$3	$.75
22c United Way	$1.25	$.20
22c Flag & Fireworks	$1	$.20
(25c) "E" & Earth	$1	$.20
25c Flag & Clouds	$1	$.20
(25c) "E" & Earth, coil	$1	$.20

1987-88	Unused	Used
25c Flag Over Yosemite	$1	$.20
25c Honey Bee	$1.20	$.20

Booklets		
(25c) "E" & Earth, booklet	$1.25	$.20
25c Pheasants, booklet	$1.20	$.20
25c Grosbeak, booklet	$1.25	$.20
25c Owl, booklet	$1.25	$.20
Grosbeak & Owl, pair	$2	$.30
25c Flag & Clouds, booklet	$1.25	$.20

1987		
North American Wildlife, pane of 50	$90	---
Any single	$1.85	$.75

1987-90 Ratification of the Constitution		
22c Delaware	$2.50	$.20
22c Pennsylvania	$2.50	$.25
22c New Jersey	$2.50	$.25
22c Georgia	$2.50	$.35
22c Connecticut	$2.50	$.25
22c Massachusetts	$2.50	$1

22c Love

22c Sojourner Truth

22c Republic of Texas

22c Duke Ellington

Fish booklet, pane of 5

1987-90 Ratification of the Constitution	Unused	Used
22c Maryland	$2.50	$.50
25c South Carolina	$2.50	$.25
25c New Hampshire	$1.95	$.25
25c Virginia	$2.50	$.25
25c New York	$2.50	$.25
25c North Carolina	$2.50	$.25
25c Rhode Island	$2.50	$.25
1987		
22c U.S.-Morocco	$2	$.20
22c William Faulkner	$2.25	$.20
American Folk Art, Lacemaking, block of 4	$6.25	---
22c Any single: Squash Blossom; Big Flower, point at top; Big Flower, scallop at top; Dogwood Blossom	$1.60	$.35
Drafting of the Constitution booklet, pane of 5	$14.95	---
22c Any single: "The Bicentennial…", "We the people…", "Establish justice…", "And secure …", "Do ordain …"	$3	$.25
22c Signing of the Constitution	$2.50	$.20
22c Certified Public Accounting	$2.95	$.20

1987	Unused	Used
Locomotives booklet, pane of 5	$10	---
22c Any single: Stourbridge Lion, Best Friend of Charleston, John Bull, Brother Jonathan, Gowan & Marx	$2	$.25
22c Christmas, Madonna	$1.25	$.20
22c Christmas, Ornaments	$1.10	$.20

1988	Unused	Used
22c Winter Olympics, Skiing	$1.25	$.20
22c Australia Bicentennial	$1.10	$.20
22c James Weldon Johnson	$1.10	$.30
Cats, block of 4	$9.95	---
22c Any single: Siamese & Exotic Shorthair, Abyssinian & Himalayan, Maine Coon & Burmese, American Shorthair & Persian	$2.50	$1
22c Knute Rockne	$1.50	$.50
25c Francis Ouimet	$1.75	$.30
25c Love, Little Rose	$1.25	$.20
45c Love, Big Roses	$2.50	$.25
25c Summer Olympics, Rings	$1.25	$.20
Classic Automobiles booklet, pane of 5	$14.50	---

Ameripex '86 Sheetlets of Presidents, set of 4

Arctic Explorers, block of 4

22c Statue of Liberty

22c T. S. Eliot

1988	Unused	Used
25c Any single: Locomobile, Pierce-Arrow, Cord, Packard, Duesenberg	$3	$.20
Antarctic Explorers, block of 4	$7.95	---
25c Any single: Nathaniel Palmer, Lt. Charles Wilkes, Richard E. Byrd, Lincoln Ellsworth	$2	$.50
American Folk Arts, Carousel Animals, block of 4	$7.95	---

American Folk Art Carved Figures, block of 4

22c Flag & Fireworks

(25c) "E" & Earth

25c Flag & Clouds

25c Honey Bee

25c Pheasants

25c Flag & Clouds

Grosbeak & Owl, pair

American Folk Art, Lacemaking, block of 4

1988	Unused	Used
25c Any single: Deer, Horse, Camel, Goat	$2	$.25
8.75 Express Mail, Eagle Obscuring Moon	$27	$14
Special Occasions (Happy & Best) booklet, pane of 6	$10.50	---
25c Either single: Happy Birthday, Best Wishes	$1.75	$.50
Special Occasions (Thinking & Love) booklet, pane of 6	$10.50	---
25c Thinking of You	$1.75	$.50
25c Love You	$1.75	$.50
25c Christmas, Madonna & Child	$1.25	$.20
25c Christmas, Sleigh Scene	$1.25	$.20

Cats, block of 4

*22c
Knute
Rockne*

*Classic Automobiles booklet,
pane of 5*

*Steamboats booklet,
pane of 5*

1989-1994

THE SELF-STICK ERA BEGINS

The most revolutionary technological advance in United States postage stamp production since perforations was the use of self-adhesives, starting in 1989 with an Eagle-and-Shield stamp sold at 15 cities throughout the country. Even a self-adhesive plastic stamp was tried in 1990. The mailing public loved the convenience of self-stick stamps, and by the end of the 1990s most stamps were issued that way.

Stamp collectors were not so accepting because the pressure-sensitive adhesive did not dissolve as the traditional lick-and-stick gum did, so used stamps could be more difficult to remove from envelopes. Specialists, however, loved the die cuts that simulated the familiar perforations and created collectible varieties, based on the arrangement of the perfs.

Another practice that affected the hobby was the increasing use of multi-stamp sets, sometimes on illustrated panes, which encouraged people to save mint stamps in panes but made the discovery of individual stamps on letters more difficult. In addition, the use of the Internet to communicate with friends and pay bills reduced markedly the use of stamps in general.

1989	Unused	Used
25c Montana Statehood	$1.50	$.20
25c A. Philip Randolph	$1.20	$.20
25c North Dakota Statehood	$1.20	$.20
25c Washington Statehood	$1.50	$.20
Steamboats booklet, pane of 5	$10.45	---
25c Any single: Experiment, Phoenix, New Orleans, Washington, Walk in the Water	$2.25	$.20
25c World Stamp Expo '89	$1.30	$.20
25c Arturo Toscanini	$1.50	$.20
Constitution Bicentennial		
25c House of Representatives	$1.30	$.20
25c Senate	$1.40	$.20
25c Executive Branch	$1.30	$.20
25c Supreme Court	$1.70	$.20
1989		
25c South Dakota Statehood	$1.30	$.20
25c Lou Gehrig	$1.30	$.20
25c Ernest Hemingway	$1.30	$.20
$2.40 Moon Landing	$14.95	$11.95

1989	Unused	Used
25c Letter Carriers	$1.20	$.20
25c Bill of Rights	$2	$.20
Prehistoric Animals, block of 4	$6.95	---
25c Any single: Tyrannosaurus Rex, Pteranodon, Stegosaurus, and Brontosaurus	$1.75	$.20
25c Pre-Columbian Figure	$1.20	$.20

(An airmail stamp of 1989 is considered part of this set.)

25c Best Wishes

25c Letter Carriers

25c World Stamp Expo '89

25c Arturo Toscanini

25c Ernest Hemingway

25c Christmas, Madonna & Child

25c Christmas, Sleigh

1989	Unused	Used
25c Christmas, Madonna & Child	$1.20	$.20
25c Christmas, Sleigh	$1.20	$.20
25c Christmas, Sleigh (booklet)	$2.75	$.20

*25c
Lou
Gehrig*

1989	Unused	Used
25c Eagle & Shield, straight borders, self-adhesive	$1.25	$1.25
World Stamp Expo souvenir sheet of 4 Lincoln stamps, imperforate	$30	---
Universal Postal Union, block of 4	$8	---
25c Any single: Stagecoach, Paddlewheel Steamer, Biplane, Automobile	$2	$.25

1989	Unused	Used
Universal Postal Union souvenir sheet, same designs, imperforate	$10	---

1990	Unused	Used
25c Idaho Statehood	$2	$.20
25c Love	$2	$.20
25c Love, booklet	$2.25	$.20
25c Ida B. Wells	$2.25	$.20
15c Beach Umbrella	$.90	$.30
25c Wyoming Statehood	$2.50	$.20
Classic Films, block of 4	$14.95	---
25c Any single: "Wizard of Oz," "Gone With the Wind," "Beau Geste," "Stagecoach"	$3.75	$.30
25c Marianne Moore	$2.50	$.20

1990-95 Transportation Coils		
4c Steam Carriage, claret	$.25	$.20
5c Circus Wagon (05), carmine on cream	$.25	$.20
5c Circus Wagon (05), carmine on white	$.20	$.20
5c Circus Wagon (5c), carmine, 1995	$.20	$.20
5c Canoe, brown	$.25	$.20

1990-95 Transportation Coils	Unused	Used
5c Canoe, red	$.25	$.20
10c Tractor Trailer, green on cream	$.50	$.20
10c Tractor Trailer, green on white	$1	$.80
20c Cog Railway, green	$1	$.30
23c Lunch Wagon, dark blue	$.95	$.20
32c Ferry Boat, blue	$1.50	$.20
$1 Seaplane, blue & scarlet	$3.95	$3.50
1990		
Lighthouses, booklet pane of 5	$14.95	---
25c Any single: Admiralty Head, Cape Hatteras, West Quoddy Head, American Shoals, Sandy hook	$3.75	$.20
25c Flag Design on plastic, self-adhesive	$2.50	$2.25
1990-95 Flora & Fauna Regular Issue		
1c Kestral (01)	$.20	$.20
1c Kestral (1c)	$.20	$.20
3c Eastern Bluebird	$.20	$.20
19c Fawn	$.45	$.20
30c Cardinal	$1.30	$.60
45c Pumpkinseed Sunfish	$1.50	$.90
$2 Bobcat	$7.95	$1

25c Eagle & Shield, self-adhesive

15c Beach Umbrella

5c Circus Wagon, coil, pair

$1 Seaplane, blue & scarlet, coil, pair

*25c Flag Design on plastic,
self-adhesive*

1c Kestral (01)

1990-95 Flora & Fauna Regular Issue	Unused	Used
20c Blue Jay, booklet	$.80	$.35
29c Wood Duck (black "29"), booklet	$1.10	$.20
29c Wood Duck (red "29"), booklet	$1.10	$.20
29c African Violets, booklet	$1.20	$.20
Peach & Pear, booklet, 10 x 11		
32c Peach (small 1995), booklet	$1.40	$.20
32c Pear (small 1995), booklet	$1.40	$.20
Peach & Pear, pair	$2.90	$.40
29c Red Squirrel, booklet	$1.10	$.40
29c Red Rose, booklet	$1.10	$.20
29c Pine Cone, booklet	$1.10	$.20
32c Pink Rose, booklet	$1.20	$.20
Peach & Pear, booklet, die cut 8.8		
32c Peach (large 1995), booklet	$1.25	$.20
32c Pear (large 1995), booklet	$1.25	$.20
Peach & Pear, pair	$2.50	$.30
1995 Coil		
32c Peach, self-adhesive	$4	$4
32c Pear, self-adhesive	$4	$4
Peach & Pear, pair	$8	---

1c Kestral (1c)

3c Eastern Bluebird

19c Fawn

30c Cardinal

$2 Bobcat

45c Pumpkinseed Sunfish

20c Blue Jay

29c African Violet

Peach & Pear, pair

29c Red Squirrel

29c Red Rose

29c Pine Cone

32c Pink Rose

Peach & Pear, pair, self-adhesive

1990	Unused	Used
Olympics, strip of 5	$10.95	---
25c Any single: Jesse Owens, Ray Ewry, Hazel Wightman, Eddie Eagan, Helene Madison	$7.95	$2.50
Indian Headdresses, strip of 5	$16.95	---
25c Any single: Assiniboine, Cheyenne, Comanche, Flathead, and Shoshone	$3.20	$.20
25c Micronesia	$1.75	$.20
25c Marshall Islands	$1.75	$.20
25c Micronesia, Marshall Islands, pair	$3.50	---
Creatures of the Sea, block of 4	$8.50	---
25c Any single: Killer Whale, Sea Lions, Sea Otter, and Dolphins	$2.15	$.20
25c Grand Canyon	$2	$.20
25c Dwight D. Eisenhower	$2	$.20
25c Christmas, Madonna & Child	$2	$.20
25c Christmas, Tree, blue-green trim	$1.75	$.20
25c Christmas, Tree, yellow-green trim (booklet)	$3	$.20
1991		
(29c) "F" & Flower	$1.30	$.20

25c Micronesia and Marshall Islands

Creatures of the Sea, block of 4

25c Grand Canyon

25c Christmas, Tree, yellow-green trim (booklet)

25c Christmas, Tree, blue-green trim

1991	Unused	Used
(29c) "F" & Flower, coil	$1.30	$.20
(29c) "F" & Flower, booklet, distinct black in leaf	$1.30	$.20
(29c) "F" & Flower, booklet, less distinct black	$6.95	$2
(4c) "This U.S. stamp…" text	$.30	$.20

(29c) "F" & Flower

(29c) "F" & Flower, coil

29c Flower, booklet,

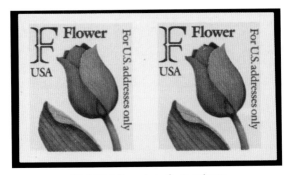

(29c) "F" & Flower, imperforate coil error

29c Flower	*29c Flower, coil (rouletted)*	*29c Flower, coil*

1991	Unused	Used
(29c) "F" & Flag Design on plastic, self-adhesive (sold only at ATM in Seattle)	$2	$.50
29c Flag Over Mt. Rushmore coil, light brown	$1.30	$.20
29c Flag Over Mt. Rushmore coil, dark brown	$1.30	$1
29c Flower	$1.30	$.20
29c Flower coil (rouletted)	$1.30	$.20
29c Flower coil	$1.30	$.80
29c Flower booklet	$1.30	$.20
29c Flag & Olympics Rings	$1.30	$.20
19c Fishing Boat coil	$.80	$.20
19c Fishing Boat coil (one loop of rope on pier)	$.80	$.60

1991	Unused	Used
19c Balloon, booklet	$.80	$.20
29c Three Flags	$1.30	$.20
29c Torch (sold only in Seattle ATM)	$1.60	$.20
50c Switzerland	$2.60	$.50
29c Vermont Statehood	$1.75	$.20
29c Savings Bonds	$1.30	$.20
29c Love, Heart-Globe, perforation 12-1/2 x 13	$1.75	$.20
29c Love, perforation 11	$1.30	$.20
29c Love, perforation 11 booklet	$2	$.20
52c Love Birds	$2.85	$.40
29c Wiliam Saroyan	$1.30	$.20
$1 Eagle & Olympics Rings	$3.95	$2.50
$2.90 Eagle Priority	$14.95	$6.95
$9.95 Eagle Express Mail	$29.95	$12.95
$14 Eagle International Express	$39.95	$9.95
$2.90 Fantasy Space Vehicle	$10.95	$2.50
$3 Challenger shuttle	$9.50	$2.25
$10.75 Endeavor Launch	$25.95	$7.95
Fishing flies booklet, pane of 5	$18	---

29c Flag & Olympics Rings

(4c) "This U.S. stamp..." text

(29c) "F" & Flag Design on plastic, self-adhesive

19c Fishing Boat, coil

19c Fishing Boat, coil
(one loop of rope on pier)

29c Three Flags

29c Torch

29c Love, Heart-Globe, perforation 12-1/2 x 13

$2.90 Eagle Priority

$1 Eagle & Olympics Rings

$9.95 Eagle Express Mail

1991	Unused	Used
29c Any single: Royal Wulff, Jock Scott, Apte Tarpon Fly, Lefty's Deceiver, Muddler Minow	$3.65	$.20
29c Cole Porter	$1.30	$.20
29c Desert Storm	$1.30	$.20
29c Desert Storm booklet	$2	$.25
Summer Olympics, strip of 5	$9.95	---
29c Any single: Pole Vault, Discus, Sprint, Javelin, Hurdles	$2	$.50
29c Numismatics	$1.50	$.20
World War II 1941 sheetlet	$15.95	---
29c Basketball	$1.50	$.25
29c District of Columbia	$1.50	$.20
Comedians, strip of 5	$13	---
29c Any single: Laurel & Hardy, Edgar Bergen & Charlie McCarthy, Jack Benny, Fannie Brice, Abbott & Costello	$2.60	$.40
29c Jan E. Matzeliger	$1.50	$.30
Space Exploration booklet, pane of 10	$25	---
29c Any single: Mercury, Venus, Earth, Moon, Mars, Jupiter, Saturn, Uranus, Neptune, Pluto	$2.50	$.30

$14 Eagle International Express

$2.90 Fantasy Space Vehicle

$10.75 Endeavor Launch

Fishing flies booklet, pane of 5

29c Desert Storm

29c Numismatics

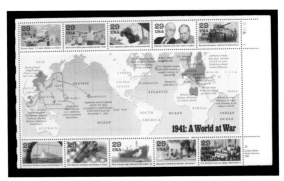

World War II 1941 sheetlet

1991	Unused	Used
(29c) Christmas, Madonna & Child	$1.40	$.20
(29c) Christmas, Santa in Chimney	$1.30	$.20
Christmas Santa booklets		
(29c) Christmas, Santa in Chimney	$3	$.50
(29c) Christmas, Santa upper left brick missing	$3	$.50
(29c) Christmas, Santa, pair, one with all bricks, one with one brick missing	$6.50	$5
29c Christmas, Checking List	$2.25	$.20
29c Christmas, With Presents	$2.25	$.20
29c Christmas, at Fireplace	$2.25	$.20
29c Christmas, Santa in Sleigh	$2.25	$.20

DIFFERENCES ABOUND

In the last decade of the 20th century the United States Postal Service produced an almost dizzying array of stamps that collectors distinguished even if the USPS did not. Each of several printers used to produce the stamps had their own standards. They used similar designs with different colors. They produced traditional stamps with water-activated adhesive and standard perforating devices or a new technology that ground the paper away to make holes. Or they produced self-adhesive stamps with the same designs for sheet stamps, booklets of various sizes or coils. Sometimes collectors can't tell one from another. Sometimes same-design stamps will have a different number of peaks or valleys on the serpentine die cuts intended to simulate perforations—or the way they meet at the corners will be different. The year dates at the bottom left of stamps since 1995 can be small or large and printed in different inks. The phosphorescent tagging is different.

Collectors can face this plethora of varieties as a challenge to be conquered or as a muddle to be avoided. Either way, they must be wary. Only the very basic different stamps are listed here. To delve deeper, seek credible guidance or at least use an authoritative, specialized catalog.

1992	Unused	Used
29c "I Pledge Allegiance," black denomination	$1.30	$.20
29c "I Pledge Allegiance," red denomination	$1.30	$.20
29c Eagle & Shield, brown denomination	$1.30	$.20
29c Eagle & Shield, green denomination	$1.30	$.20
29c Eagle & Shield, red denomination	$1.30	$.20
(10c) Bulk Rate USA Eagle & Shield	$.50	$.20
(10c) USA Bulk Rate	$.50	$.20
(10c) USA Bulk Rate, metallic gold	$.50	$.20
23c Flag & "Presorted"	$1	$.30
23c USA reflecting flag, coils (three versions)	$1	$.20
29c Flag Over White House coil	$1.30	$.20
Winter Olympics, strip of 5	$6.95	---
29c Any single: Hockey, Figure Skating, Speed Skating, Skiing, Bobsledding	$1.40	$.20
29c World Columbian Stamp Expo	$1.75	$.20
29c W.E.B. DuBois	$1.60	$.20
29c Love Envelope & Heart	$1.60	$.20
29c Olympics Baseball	$2	$.20
Voyage of Columbus, block of 4	$5.95	---

32c "I Pledge Allegiance," black denomination

32c "I Pledge Allegiance," red denomination

29c Eagle & Shield, brown denomination

29c Eagle & Shield, green denomination

29c Eagle & Shield, red denomination

(10c) Bulk Rate USA Eagle & Shield

(10c) USA Bulk Rate

(10c) USA Bulk Rate, metallic gold

23c Flag & "Presorted"

1992	Unused	Used
29c Any single: Meeting Queen Isabella, Crossing the Atlantic, Approaching Land, Coming Ashore	$1.50	$.20
World Columbian souvenir sheets, set of 6	$52.50	---
The souvenir sheets reproduced, on illustrated sheetlets, the Columbian Exposition stamps of 1893 but are dated "1492-1992."		
29c New York Stock Exchange	$1.50	$.20
Space Accomplishments, block of 4	$6.95	---
29c Any single: Soviet Cosmonaut, U.S. Astronaut, Apollo Spacecraft, Soyuz Spacecraft	$1.75	$.20
29c Alaska Highway	$1.30	$.20
29c Kentucky Statehood	$1.60	$.20
Summer Olympics, strip of 5	$6.95	---
29c Any single: Soccer, Women's Gymnastics, Volleyball, Boxing, Swimming	$1.40	$1
Hummingbirds booklet, pane of 5	$7.50	---
29c Any single: Ruby-Throated, Broad-Billed, Costa's, Rufous, Caliope	$1.50	$.20
Wildflowers, pane of 50	$75	---
29c Any single stamp	$1.50	$.75
World War II 1942, sheetlet of 10	$15.95	---
29c Any single stamp	$1.50	$1.20

29c Flag Over White
House, coil

29c World Columbian
Stamp Expo

29c W.E.B. DuBois

29c Love

29c Olympics Baseball

1992	Unused	Used
29c Dorothy Parker	$1.95	$.20
29c Dr. Theodore Von Karman	$1.30	$.20
Minerals, block of 4	$5.95	---
29c Any single: Azurite, Copper, Variscite, Wulfenite	$1.50	$.20
29c Juan Cabrillo	$1.60	$.20

Voyage of Columbus, block of 4

Hummingbirds booklet, pane of 5

World War II 1942, sheetlet of 10

1992	Unused	Used
Wild Animals booklet, pane of 5	$7.50	---
29c Any single: Giraffe, Panda, Flamingo, King Penguin, White Bengal Tiger	$1.50	$.20
29c Christmas, Madonna & Child	$1.30	$.20
Christmas Toys, block of 4 ("Greetings" 27 mm)	$6.95	---
29c Any single: Horse & Rider, Train Engine, Fire Pumper, Riverboat	$1.75	$.20
Christmas Toys booklet ("Greetings" 25 mm)	$10.95	---
29c Same designs, each	$2.75	$.20
29c Christmas, Train booklet, self-adhesive ("Greetings" 21-1/2 mm)	$1.50	$1.45
29c Year of the Rooster	$1.50	$.20

LONG LIVE THE KING

The most popular stamp in United States history is the 1993 commemorative issue for Elvis Presley, "The King of Rock 'n' Roll."

Prior to its production, the public voted to select the stamp design from two likenesses of the singer—young and more mature—and each postcard ballot had to bear a stamp. All told, 1,128,923 ballots were cast (at a postage cost of $214,495.37), and the "Young Elvis" won, by a 3-1 margin. There were 517 million Elvis stamps released in January 1993. An additional 113 million stamps with his likeness and full name were produced on booklet and sheet stamps for the Rock 'n Roll/Rhythm & Blues set that same year to kick off the new American Music commemorative series, which ran until 1999. USPS surveys indicated that 124 million Elvis stamps sold would be saved, not used on mail.

29c Elvis

1993	Unused	Used
29c Elvis (Presley)	$1.50	$.20
29c Oklahoma!	$1.30	$.20
29c Hank Williams, perforation 10, 27-1/2 mm inscription, two tuning keys on guitar	$2	$.20
29c Hank Williams, perforation 11.2 x 11.5	$45	$25
Rock 'n' Roll & Rhythm and Blues, vertical strip of 7, no frame lines	$15.95	---
29c Elvis Presley	$4	$3.50
29c Bill Haley	$1.75	$1.75
29c Clyde McPhatter	$2	$1.75
29c Ritchie Valens	$2	$1.75
29c Otis Redding	$2.75	$2.50
29c Buddy Holly	$2.25	$1.75
29c Dinah Washington	$2	$1.75
Rock 'n' Roll & Rhythm and Blues, booklet, vertical strip of 7, with frame lines	$10.95	---
29c Elvis Presley	$2	$.40
29c Bill Haley	$1.50	$.40
29c Clyde McPhatter	$1.50	$.40
29c Ritchie Valens	$1.50	$.30
29c Otis Redding	$1.50	$.25

1993	Unused	Used
29c Buddy Holly	$1.50	$.25
29c Dinah Washington	$1.50	$.25
Space Fantasy booklet, pane of 5	$7	---
29c Any single: Ringed Planet, Saucer-Shaped Craft, Astronauts, Craft With Long Wings, Craft With Short Wings	$1.40	$.20
29c Percy Lavon Julian	$1.30	$.20
29c Oregon Trail	$1.85	$.20
29c World University Games	$1.30	$.20
29c Grace Kelly	$1.50	$.20
Circus, block of 4	$10.95	---
29c Any single: Clown, Ringmaster, Trapeze Artist, Elephant	$2.75	$.30
29c Cherokee Strip Land Run	$1.20	$.20
29c Dean Acheson	$1.50	$.20
Sporting Horses, block of 4	$7	---
29c Any single: Steeplechase, Thoroughbred, Harness, Polo	$1.75	$1.25
Garden Flowers booklet, pane of 5	$8.95	---
29c Any single: Hyacinth, Daffodil, Tulip Iris, Lilac	$1.80	$.20
World War II, 1943 sheetlet	$20	---
29c Any single	$1.75	$1

1993	Unused	Used
29c Joe Louis	$1.50	$.20
Broadway Musicals booklet, pane of 4	$10.95	---
29c Show Boat	$2.60	$.20
29c Porgy & Bess	$3.20	$.20
29c Oklahoma!	$2.60	$.20
29c My Fair Lady	$2.60	$.20
Country Music Legends, block of 4	$12.95	---
29c Any single: Hank Williams, 27 mm inscription, parts of four tuning keys on guitar, Patsy Cline, Carter Family, Bob Wills	$3.25	$3
Country Music Legends, booklet strip	$5.95	---
29c Any single: Hank Williams (22 mm inscription), Carter Family, Patsy Cline, Bob Wills	$1.50	$.25
National Postal Museum, block of 4	$9	---
29c Any single: Benjamin Franklin, Civil War Soldier, Charles Lindbergh, Classic Stamps	$2.25	$1.50
American Sign Language, pair	$3.60	$.40
29c Either single: Mother & Baby, Sign for "I Love You"	$1.80	$.20
Children's Classic Books, block of 4	$10	---

29c Hank Williams, perforation 10, 27-1/2 mm inscription, two tuning keys on guitar

29c Elvis Presley

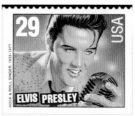

29c Elvis Presley, from booklet, with frame lines

1993	Unused	Used
29c Any single: Rebecca of Sunnybrook Farm, Little House on the Prairie, Adventures of Huckleberry Finn, Little Women	$2.50	$.75
29c Christmas, Madonna & Child	$1.30	$.20
29c Christmas, Madonna & Child, booklet	$1.30	$.20

29c Buddy Holly

Broadway Musicals booklet,
pane of 4

29c Grace Kelly

Country Music Legends

1993	Unused	Used
Christmas, Symbols & Snow, block of 4, perforation 11-1/2	$8	---
29c Any single: Jack-in-the-Box, Reindeer, Snowman (three buttons, seven flakes under nose) Toy Soldier	$1.90	$.20
Christmas, Symbols & Snow, booklet block of 4, Perforation 11 x 10	$5.95	---

Silent Screen Stars, block of 10

1993	Unused	Used
29c Any single: Toy Soldier, Snowman (two buttons, five flakes under nose), Reindeer, Jack-in-the-Box	$1.50	$.20
Christmas, Symbols & Snow, booklet, self-adhesive, imperforate block of 4	$5.95	---
29c Any single: Snowman (three buttons, seven flakes under nose), Toy Soldier, Jack-in-the-Box, Reindeer	$1.50	$.20
29c Christmas Snowman (two buttons, four snowflakes under nose), booklet, self-adhesive, imperforate	$1.50	$1.25

1993	Unused	Used
29c Mariana Islands	$1.30	$.20
29c Columbus Landing in Puerto Rico	$1.30	$.20
29c AIDS Awareness	$1.30	$.20
1994		
Winter Olympics, strip of 5	$8.50	---
29c Any single: Slalom, Luge, Ice Dancing, Cross-Country Skiing, Ice Hockey	$1.70	$1.30
29c Edward R. Murrow	$1.60	$.20
29c Love, Heart & Horizon, self-adhesive	$1.75	$.20
29c Love, Dove in Heart	$1.30	$.20
29c Love, Dove in Heart booklet	$1.95	$.20
52c Love, Bouquet & Dove	$2.75	$.25
29c Dr. Allison Davis	$1.75	$.20
29c Year of the Dog	$2.50	$.20
29c Buffalo Soldiers	$1.75	$.20
Silent Screen Stars, block of 10	$24	---
29c Rudolph Valentino	$2.50	$2.15
29c Clara Bow	$2.50	$2.15
29c Charles Chaplin	$2.75	$2.50
29c Lon Chaney	$2.50	$2.15

29c Eagle & Stripes

29c Statue of Liberty

29c Norman Rockwell

$9.95 Moon Landing

29c James Thurber

Popular Singers, vertical strip of 5

Cranes, pair

1994	Unused	Used
29c Eagle & Stripes	$1.30	$.20
29c Statue of Liberty	$1.50	$.20
$1 Surrender of Burgoyne	$3.95	$.50
$5 George Washington & Andrew Jackson	$14.95	$2.95
29c John Gilbert	$2.50	$2.15
29c Zasu Pitts	$2.95	$2.50
29c Harold Lloyd	$2.50	$2.15
29c Keystone Kops	$2.50	$2.15
29c Theda Bara	$2.50	$2.25
29c Buster Keaton	$2.95	$2.50
Garden Flowers booklet, pane of 5	$7.95	---
29c Any single: Lily, Zinnia, Gladiola, Marigold, Rose	$1.60	$.20
29c World Cup Soccer, Kicking	$1.50	$.20
40c World Cup Soccer, Trapping	$2.25	$2
50c World Cup Soccer, Heading	$2.75	$2.60
World Cup Soccer, souvenir sheet of 3	$15	---
World War II 1944, sheetlet of 10	$34.95	---
29c Any single	$3.50	$1
29c Norman Rockwell	$1.50	$.20

1994	Unused	Used
Rockwell's Four Freedoms, sheetlet	$10.95	---
50c Any single: Freedom From Want, Freedom From Fear, Freedom of Speech, Freedom Of Worship	$2.75	$1
29c Moon Landing	$1.75	$.25
$9.95 Moon Landing	$29	$10
Locomotives booklet, pane of 5	$8.95	---
29c Any single: Hudson's General, McQueen's Jupiter, Eddy's No. 242, Ely's No. 10, Buchanan's No. 999	$1.80	$.20
29c George Meany	$1.75	$.20
Popular Singers, vertical strip of 5	$7.95	---
29c Any single: Al Jolson, Bing Crosby, Ethel Waters, Nat "King" Cole, Ethel Merman	$1.60	$1.60
Blues & Jazz Singers, irregular block of 10	$14.00	---
29c Bessie Smith	$1.50	$1.30
29c Muddy Waters	$1.50	$1.30
29c Billie Holiday	$1.30	$1.30
29c Robert Johnson	$2	$1.85
29c Jimmy Rushing	$2.50	$1.20
29c "Ma" Rainey	$2	$1.20
29c Mildred Bailey	$1.75	$1.20
29c Howlin' Wolf	$2.25	$1.85

1994	Unused	Used
29c James Thurber	$1.75	$.20
Wonders of the Sea, block of 4	$6.95	---
29c Any single: Motorboat, Ship, Ship's Wheel, Coral	$1.75	$1.25
Cranes, pair	$2.60	$.60
29c Black-Necked or Whooping Crane	$1.30	$.25
Legends of the West, pane of 20 (with error)	$300	---
Legends of the West, pane (thicker frame lines)	$40	---
29c Any single stamp	$1.75	$.50
29c Christmas, Madonna & Child, perforation 11	$1.50	$.20
29c Christmas, Madonna & Child, booklet	$1.60	$.20
29c Christmas, Stocking, perforation 11-3/4	$2	$.20
29c Christmas, Santa Claus, self-adhesive booklet	$1.75	$.20
29c Christmas, Cardinal, self-adhesive booklet	$1.85	$1.75
Bureau of Engraving & Printing souvenir sheet	$25	---
$2 J. Madison (design from early BEP stamp)	$4	$2
29c Year of the Boar	$1.95	$1.75

$1 Surrender of Burgoyne

1994 Definitives for New Postal Rate	Unused	Used
(3c) Dove of Peace (light or heavy inscription)	$.20	$.20
(20c) Flag & black "G Postcard"	$1.10	$.20
(20c) Flag & red "G Postcard"	$1.10	$.20
(32c) Flag & black "G For U.S. Addresses"	$2.50	$1.50
32c Flag & red "G For U.S."	$1.60	$.20
(32c) Flag & black "G," booklet, perforation 10 x 9.9	$1.30	$.20
(32c) Flag & blue "G", booklet	$1.50	$.20
(32c) Flag & red "G" slightly lower than on sheet stamp	$2.25	$.20

1994	Unused	Used
(32c) Flag & black "G", booklet (also coil, little blue shading in white stripes below stars)	$1.30	$.25
(32c) Flag & black "G" (noticeable blue shading in white stripes below stars)	$1.30	$.50
(25c) Flag & black "G" on blue background, coil	$1.20	$.65
(32c) Flag & black "G For U.S.", coil	$3	$.50
(32c) Flag & blue "G", coil	$1.20	$.20
(32c) Flag & red "G", coil	$1.50	$.20
(32c) Flag & red "G" rouletted vertically, coil	$1.20	$.20

$5 George Washington & Andrew Jackson

1995-2010

'POP' GOES THE POSTAGE

The use of staid and somber images of deceased American statesmen on its stamps had long since been dropped but, from 1995 on, the U.S. Postal Service enthusiastically embraced popular culture on its issues.

Marilyn Monroe kicked off an annual Legends of Hollywood series. A Comic Strip Classics sheetlet led to a series of Warner Bros. cartoon characters, starting with Bugs Bunny, and then Disney cartoon characters and others.

Musicians, songwriters, artists, and movie and television stars appeared in abundance on stamps. Athletes and even playing fields found a home there. The environment, endangered species, outer space and social and medical causes appeared.

Holograms were used on a set of souvenir sheets in 1997.

As the first decade of the 21st century ended, "forever" stamps, which would be valid for first-class mailing even when postage rates increased, seemed to gain a foothold.

1995	Unused	Used
(5c) Flag & "G Nonprofit Presort" on green, coil	$.75	$.50
32c Flag Over Porch	$1.20	$.20
32c James K. Polk	$1.30	$.20
1995-97 Coils		
(5c) Buttes, Non-Profit	$.35	$.20
(5c) Buttes, self-adhesive	$.35	$.20
(10c) Mountains, purplish	$.35	$.20
(10c) Mountains, bluish	$.35	$.20
(10c) Mountains, self-adhesive, purplish	$.35	$.20
(10c) Mountains, self-adhesive, bluish	$.35	$.20
(10c) Auto, Bulk Rate	$.50	$.20
(10c) Auto, self-adhesive	$.50	$.20
(10c) Eagle & Shield, self-adhesive	$.40	$.20
(15c) Tail Fin, bold colors, heavy shading	$.60	$.25
(15c) Tail Fin, subdued colors, finer detail	$.60	$.25
(15c) Tail Fin, self-adhesive	$.70	$.25
(25c) Juke Box, self-adhesive, die cut 11.5	$1	$.50
(25c) Juke Box, dark blue in music box	$1	$.25
(25c) Juke Box, bright, light blue in music box	$1	$.25
(25c) Juke Box, self-adhesive, die cut 9.8	$1	$.40

1995-97 Coils	Unused	Used
(25c) Juke Box with simulated perforations, liner-less	$1	$.60
32c Flag Over Porch, red 1995, perforation 9.8	$1.25	$2
32c Flag Over Porch, blue 1995	$1.25	$2
32c Flag Over Porch, self-adhesive, blue 1995	$1.25	$.75
32c Flag Over Porch, S-A, red 1996	$2.50	$.75
32c Flag Over Porch, S-A, blue 1996	$1.25	$.50
Booklets		
32c Flag Over Porch, red 1995	$1	$.25
32c Flag Over Field, self-adhesive	$1.50	$.50
32c Flag Over Porch, S-A, large date, blue 1995	$2	$.40
32c Flag Over Porch, S-A, liner-less, blue 1996	$1.30	$1.25
1995-99 Great Americans Series		
32c Milton S. Hershey	$1.20	$.50
32c Cal Farley	$1.25	$.20
32c Henry R. Luce	$1.25	$.50
32c Lila & DeWitt Wallace	$1.25	$.70
46c Ruth Benedict	$2	$1

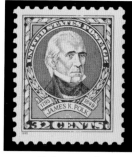

32c James K. Polk

32c Flag Over Porch

(5c) Buttes, Non-Profit

(10c) Mountains, purplish

(10c) Auto,
Bulk Rate

(15c) Tail Fin,
bold colors,
heavy shading

(15c) Tail Fin,
subdued colors,
finer detail

(25c) Juke Box,
dark blue in music box

(25c) Juke Box, bright,
light blue in music box

1995-99 Great Americans Series	Unused	Used
55c Dr. Alice Hamilton	$2	$.20
55c Justin S. Morrill, self-adhesive	$2.20	$.50
77c Mary Breckinridge, self-adhesive	$2.50	$1
78c Alice Paul	$3.50	$2
1995		
(32c) Love Cherub, large vertical	$1	$.20
(32c) Love Cherub, self-adhesive	$1	$.20
32c Florida Statehood	$1	$.20
Earth Day, block of 4	$5	---
32c Any single: Earth in Tub, Solar Energy, Tree Planting, Beach Cleanup	$1	$.20
32c Richard M. Nixon	$1.25	$.20
32c Bessie Coleman	$1.50	$.30
32c Love Cherub, vertical	$1.25	$.20
55c Love Cherub, horizontal	$2.20	$.50
32c Love Cherub, vertical, booklet	$1.25	$.25
55c Love Cherub, horizontal, self-adhesive	$2.20	$.50
Recreational Sports, vertical strip of 5	$6.25	---
32c Any single: Volleyball, Softball, Bowling, Tennis, Golf	$1.25	$.50
32c Prisoner of War/Missing in Action	$1.25	$.20

1995	Unused	Used
32c Marilyn Monroe	$2.50	$.30
32c Texas Statehood	$2	.20
Great Lakes Lighthouses booklet, pane of 5	$6.25	---
32c Any single: Split Rock, St. Joseph, Spectacle Reef, Marble Head, Thirty Mile Point	$1.25	$.20
32c United Nations	$1.20	$.20
Civil War, sheetlet of 20	$45	---
32c Any single	$2	$.35
Carousel Horses, block of 4	$6.50	---
32c Any single: Gold, Black & Gold, Silver, Brown	$1.50	$.25
32c Woman Suffrage	$1.25	$.25
World War II 1945, sheetlet of 10	$22	---
32c Any single	$2	$.35
32c Louis Armstrong, white "32"	$1.50	$1
Jazz Musicians, block of 10	$35	---
32c Any single: Coleman Hawkins, Louis Armstrong (black "32"), James P. Johnson, Jelly Roll Morton, Charlie Parker, Eubie Blake, Charles Mingus, Thelonius Monk, John Coltrane, Erroll Garner	$2.50	$2
Garden Flowers booklet, pane of 5	$7	---

1995	Unused	Used
32c Any single: Aster, Chrysanthemum, Dahlia, Hydrangea, Rudbeckia	$1.25	$.20
60c Eddie Rickenbacker	$2	$.30
32c Republic of Palau	$1.25	$.20
Comic Strip Classics, sheetlet of 20	$25	---
32c Any single	$1.25	$.75
32c U.S. Naval Academy	$1	$.25
32c Tennessee Williams	$2	$.25
32c Christmas, Madonna & Child	$1	$.20
32c Christmas, Madonna & Child booklet	$1	$.20
Christmas Figures, block of 4	$4.50	---
32c Any single: Santa Claus at Chimney, Boy with Jumping Jack, Boy with Tree, Santa in Workshop	$1	$.20
Christmas Figures, self-adhesive booklet of 20	$8	---
32c Any single: Santa in Workshop, Boy with Jumping Jack, Santa at Chimney, Boy with Tree	$1	$.25
32c Christmas, Midnight Angel booklet	$1.25	$.25
32c Christmas, Sledding booklet	$2	$.75

32c Milton S. Hershey

32c Cal Farley

46c Ruth Benedict

55c Dr. Alice Hamilton

78c Alice Paul

32c Love Cherub, vertical

32c Marilyn Monroe

60c Eddie Rickenbacker

Self-Adhesive Coils (sold only through mail order)	Unused	Used
Christmas Figures, strip of 4 (Santa in Workshop, Boy with Jumping Jack, Santa at Chimney, Boy with Tree)	$5	---
32c Any single	$1	$.25

1995		
32c Christmas, Midnight Angel, coil	$1.25	$1.25
Antique Automobiles, strip of 5	$7.50	---
32c Any single: Duryea, Haynes, Columbia, Winton, White	$1.25	$.75

1996		
32c Utah Statehood	$1	$.30
Winter Garden Flowers booklet, pane of 5	$7	---
32c Any single: Crocus, Winter Aconite, Pansy, Snowdrop, Anemone	$1.25	$.20
32c Love Cherub, self-adhesive	$.90	$.20

1996-2000 Flora & Fauna Series		
1c Kestral "1c" self-adhesive, die-cut 10-1/2	$.20	$.20
1c Kestral "1c" self-adhesive, die-cut 11-1/2, blue inscription and year	$.20	$.20

1996-2000 Flora & Fauna Series	Unused	Used
2c Red-headed Woodpecker	$.20	$.20
3c Eastern Bluebird "3c"	$.20	$.20
$1 Red Fox	$3.95	$1.25
Coil Stamps		
1c Kestral "1c", coil	$.20	$.20
2c Red-headed Woodpecker, coil	$.20	$.20
1996-2000		
20c Blue Jay, booklet	$1	$.30
32c Yellow Rose, booklet	$1.20	$.25

32c Christmas, Midnight Angel

2c Red-headed Woodpecker

3c Eastern Bluebird "3c" *1c Kestral "1c"*

1996-2000	Unused	Used
20c Ring-necked Pheasant, die-cut 11-1/4, booklet	$.80	$.35
20c Ring-necked Pheasant, 10-1/2 x 11, booklet	$1.30	$1.20
33c Coral Pink Rose, 11-1/2 x 11-1/4, booklet	$1.30	$.20
20c Blue Jay, coil	$	$.30
32c Yellow Rose, coil	$1.30	$.25
20c Ring-necked Pheasant, coil	$.80	$.25
1996		
32c Ernest E. Just	$1.30	$.20
32c Smithsonian Institution	$1.30	$.20

$1 Red Fox

20c Blue Jay

32c Smithsonian Institution

32c Georgia O'Keeffe

1996	Unused	Used
32c Year of the Rat	$1.60	$.20
Pioneers of Communication, block of 4	$6	---
32c Any single: Edweard Muybridge, Ottmar Mergenthaler, Frederick E. Ives, William Dickson	$1	$.50
32c Fulbright Scholarships	$1	$.25

1996	Unused	Used
32c Jacqueline Cochran	$2	$.30
32c Marathon	$1	$.20
Olympics, pane of 20	$22	---
32c Any single	$1	$.30
32c Georgia O'Keeffe	$2	$.25
32c Tennessee Statehood, perforated	$1	$.25
32c Tennessee Statehood, self-adhesive	$1	$.25
American Indian Dances, strip of 5	$7	---
32c Any single: Fancy Dance, Butterfly Dance, Traditional Dance, Raven Dance, Hoop Dance	$1	$.75
Prehistoric Animals, block of 4	$4	---
32c Any single: Eohippus, Wooly Mammoth, Mastodon, Saber-tooth Cat	$1	$.25
32c Breast Cancer Awareness	$1.20	$.20
32c James Dean	$1.30	$.30
Folk Heroes, block of 4	$6	---
32c Any single: Mighty Casey, Paul Bunyan, John Henry, Pecos Bill	$1.50	$1
32c Olympics, Discus Thrower	$2	$.20
32c Iowa Statehood, perforated	$1	$.20
32c Iowa Statehood, self-adhesive	$1	$.20

32c Breast Cancer Awareness

32c James Dean

1996	Unused	Used
32c Rural Free Delivery	$1	$.20
Riverboats, strip of 5	$7	---
32c Any single: Robert E. Lee, Sylvan Dell, Far West, Rebecca Everingham, Bailey Gatzert	$1	$.25
Big Band Leaders, block of 4	$5	---
32c Any single: Count Basie, Tommy & Jimmy Dorsey, Glenn Miller, Benny Goodman	$1.20	$.25
Song Writers, block of 4	$5	---

Folk Heroes, block of 4

Big Band Leaders, block of 4

1996	Unused	Used
32c Any single: Harold Arlen, Johnny Mercer, Dorothy Fields, Hoagy Carmichael	$1.20	$.25
32c F. Scott Fitzgerald	$1.20	$.25
Endangered Species, pane of 15	$22	---
32c Any single	$1.20	$.50
32c Computer Technology	$1.20	$.20
32c Christmas, Madonna & Child	$1.30	$.20
Christmas Joy, perforated, block of 4	$5	---
32c Any single: Fireplace, Tree, Santa, Shopping	$1.20	$.25
32c Christmas, Madonna & Child, S-A	$1.20	$.25
Christmas Joy, self-adhesive booklet, pane of 20	$18	---
32c Any single: Fireplace, Tree, Santa, Shopping	$1.20	$.25
32c Christmas, Skating, self-adhesive	$1.25	$.75
32c Hanukkah, self-adhesive	$1.30	$.35
Cycling, souvenir sheet of 2	$3	---
50c Either single, orange or blue-green	$1.50	$1

INNOVATIONS IN 1997

Stamp innovations highlighted the year 1997. The United States issued its first triangle-shaped stamps to help promote the large international stamp show, Pacific '97, embedded hidden images or "scrambled indicia," as the USPS called them, on some stamps, and issued at the end of the year its largest postage stamp ever.

The most attention, by the public as well as by philatelists, was devoted to the appearance of the cartoon character Bugs Bunny on a postage stamp as well as on promotional material aimed at youthful collectors. Purists felt a commercial character had no place in the U.S. stamp program. But the USPS noted that the number of young collectors had plummeted from 2.5 million in 1952 to 150,000 in 1994 and instituted a "Stampers" club to encourage youths in the hobby. Some of the Bugs panes of nine stamps were specially printed with die cutting that penetrated the booklets' backing paper and allowed easy separation to send individual stamps in kits to club members. The single stamp on the right-hand pane had no die cutting at all, making it an inadvertent but deliberate "imperforate" variety that gained popularity with collectors. Hidden images, which could be seen with the aid of a special plastic lens available through the postal service, appeared for the first time—a repeated "USAF" on the Air Force stamp and appropriate icons on the individual Movie Monsters stamps. The images were used intermittently for a few years.

Another innovation was the use of the micro-printed letters "USPS" to form the entire image of the Padre Felix Varela stamp.

With dimensions of 3 x 1-1/2 inches, the Mars Pathfinder Priority Mail rate stamp was easily the largest ever issued by the U.S. It also had the hidden image word-

ing on the stamp and "USA" as part of the perforation on the bottom.

32c Pacific '97 Triangle, ship

32c Pacific '97, stagecoach

1997	Unused	Used
32c Year of the Ox	$1.20	$.20
32c Brig. Gen. Benjamin O. Davis Sr.	$1.30	$.20
32c Statue of Liberty booklet, die-cut 11	$1	$.20
32c Statue of Liberty booklet, 11.5 x 11.8	$2	$.50
32c Love Swans	$1.30	$.20
55c Love Swans	$2	$.40
32c Helping Children Learn	$1	$.20
Merian Botanical Prints, self-adhesive, pair	$2.50	---
32c Either single, 18.5 x 24 mm, Citron, Flowering Pineapple	$1.20	$.20
Pacific '97 triangles, pair	$2.50	$.50
32c Either single: Ship or Stagecoach	$1.20	$.25
32c Thornton Wilder	$1	$.20
32c Raoul Wallenberg	$1	$.20
The World of Dinosaurs, pane of 15	$18	---
32c Any single	$1	$.35
Bugs Bunny, panes of 9 and 1	$12	---
32c die-cut single stamp, backing not cut	$1	$.25
32c die-cut single, backing also cut	$4	---
32c single stamp, not die-cut	$175	---

1997	Unused	Used
Pacific '97, Franklin souvenir sheet of 12	$17	---
50c Benjamin Franklin single	$1.20	$.50
Pacific '97, Washington souvenir sheet of 12	$20	---
60c George Washington single	$1.50	$.70
32c Marshall Plan	$1	$.20
Classic American Aircraft, page of 20	$22	---
32c Any single	$1	$.25
Football Coaches, block of 4	$4	---
32c Any single: Bear Bryant, Pop Warner, Vince Lombardi, George Halas	$1	$.50
32c Vince Lombardi, red strip over name	$1	$.50
32c Bear Bryant, red strip over name	$1	$.50
32c Pop Warner, red strip over name	$1	$.50
32c George Halas, red strip over name	$1	$.50
Classic American Dolls, pane of 15	$18	---
32c Any single	$1.20	$.40
32c Humphrey Bogart	$1.20	$.30
32c Stars & Stripes Forever	$1.20	$.20
Opera Singers, block of 4	$5	---
32c Any single: Lily Pons, Richard Tucker, Lawrence Tibbett, Rosa Ponselle	$1.20	$1

1997	Unused	Used
Classical Composers and Conductors, block of 8	$12	---
Any single: Leopold Stokowski, Arthur Fiedler, George Szell, Eugene Ormandy, Samuel Barger, Ferde Grofe, Charles Ives, Louis Moreau Gottschal	$1.20	$1
32c Padre Felix Varela	$1.30	$.50
32c U.S. Air Force	$1.20	$.20
Classic Movie Monsters, strip of 5	$8	---
32c Any single: Phantom of the Opera, Dracula, Frankenstein Monster, The Mummy, Wolf Man	$1.20	$.25
32c Supersonic Flight	$1.20	$.30
32c Women in the Military	$1.20	$.20
32c Kwanzaa	$1.20	$.20
32c Christmas, Madonna & Child, S-A	$1.20	$.20
32c Christmas, Holly	$1.20	$.20
Mars Pathfinder souvenir sheet	$10	$4
$3 Mars Rover Sojourner	$9.50	$4
1998		
32c Year of the Tiger	$1.20	$.20
32c Alpine Skiing	$1.20	$.20
32c Madam C.J. Walker	$1.30	$.20
Celebrate the Century 1900s, pane of 15	$15	---

1998	Unused	Used
32c Any single	$1	$.30
Celebrate the Century 1910s, pane of 15	$15	---
32c Any single	$1	$.30
Celebrate the Century 1920s, pane of 15	$15	---
32c Any single	$1	$.30
Celebrate the Century 1930s, pane of 15	$15	---
32c Any single	$1	$.30
Celebrate the Century 1940s, pane of 15	$15	---
33c Any single	$1	$.30
Celebrate the Century 1950s, pane of 15	$15	---
33c Any single	$1	$.30
Celebrate the Century 1960s, pane of 15	$15	---
33c Any single	$1	$.30
Celebrate the Century 1970s, pane of 15	$15	---
33c Any single	$1	$.30
Celebrate the Century 1980s, pane of 15	$15	---
33c Any single	$1	$.30
Celebrate the Century 1990s, pane of 15	$15	---
33c Any single	$1	$.30
32c Remember the Maine	$1	$.20

1998	Unused	Used
Flowering Trees, strip of 5	$5	---
32c Any single: Southern Magnolia, Blue Paloverde, Yellow Poplar, Prairie Crab Apple, Pacific Dogwood	$1	$.30
Alexander Calder sheelet, strip of five	$7	---
32c Any single: Black Cascade, 13 Verticals, 1959; Untitled, 1965; Rearing Stallion, 1928; Portrait of a Young Man, c. 1945; Un Effet du Japonais, 1945	$1.20	$.30
32c Cinco de Mayo	$1.30	$.20
Sylvester & Tweety, panes of 9 and 1	$12	---
32c die-cut single stamp, backing not cut	$1	$.25
32c die-cut single, backing also cut	$4	---
32c Wisconsin Statehood	$1.20	$.30
Coil stamps		
(5c) Wetlands "Nonprofit," perforation 10	$.25	$.20
(5c) Wetlands, self-adhesive	$.25	$.20
(25c) Diner "Presorted"	$1	$.20
(25c) Diner, self-adhesive	$1	$.20

*32c
Humphrey
Bogart*

*32c
Christmas,
Holly*

*32c Cinco
de Mayo*

*(25c) Diner
"Presorted"*

Folk Musicians

Gospel Singers

1998	Unused	Used
Trans-Mississippi bi-color, sheetlet of 9	$12	---
1c Marquette on the Mississippi	$.30	$.25
2c Farming in the West	$.30	$.25
4c Indian Hunting Buffalo	$.30	$.25
5c Fremont on Rocky Mountains	$.30	$.25
8c Troops Guarding Train	$.50	$.25
10c Hardships of Emigration	$1	$.25
50c Western Mining Prospector	$2	$.40
$1 Western Cattle in a Storm	$2	$1
$2 Mississippi Bridge	$5	$2
Trans-Mississippi bi-color, sheetlet of 9 $1	$20	---
32c Berlin Airlift	$1.25	$.20
Folk Musicians, block of 4	$5	---
32c And single: Leadbelly, Woody Guthrie, Sonny Terry, Josh White	$1.20	$.30
Gospel Singers, block of 4	$5	---
32c Any single: Mahalia Jackson, Roberta Martin, Clara Ward, Sister Rosetta	$1.20	$.30
32c Spanish Settlement	$1	$.20
32c Stephen Vincent Benet	$1	$.30
Tropical Birds, block of 4	$4	---

1998	Unused	Used
32c Any single: Antillean Euphonia, Green-throated Carib, Crested Honeycreeper, Cardinal Honeyeater	$1	$.20
32c Alfred Hitchcock	$1.50	$.30
32c Organ & Tissue Donation	$1	$.30
(10c) Bicycle Handlebar, self-adhesive, coil	$.40	$.25
(10c) Bicycle Handlebar, perforated, coil	$.40	$.25
Bright Eyes, strip of 5	$4	---
32c Any single: Dog, Fish, Cat, Parakeet, Hamster	$1	$.25
32c Klondike Gold Rush	$1	$.30
Four Centuries of American Art, pane of 20	$30	---
32c Any single	$1.50	$.45
32c Ballet	$1	$.25
Space Discovery, strip of 5	$6	---
Any single: Space City, Pod-Craft in air, Person in Space Suit, Planet Rover, Spaceport Dome	$1.20	$.25
32c Giving & Sharing	$1.20	$.20
32c Christmas, Madonna & Child	$1.30	$.20
Christmas, Wreaths, S-A booklet, pane of 6	$12	---

1998	Unused	Used
32c Any single: Evergreen, Victorian, Chili Pepper, Tropical	$2	$.75
Christmas, Wreaths, S-A strip of 4 (23 x 30 mm)	$8	---
32c Any single, as above	$2	$.20

Regular Issues		
(1c) Weather Vane, white "USA"	$.20	$.20
(1c) Weather Vane, blue "USA"	$.20	$.20
22c Uncle Sam, self-adhesive	$.90	$.30
$3.20 Shuttle Landing, self-adhesive	$10	$5
$11.75 Piggyback Shuttle, self-adhesive	$27	$18

1998		
22c Uncle Sam, self-adhesive, coil	$.80	$.25
(33c) Uncle Sam's Hat "H" gummed, coil	$1.20	$.25
(33c) Hat "H," S-A, square corners, coil	$1.20	$.20
(33c) Hat "H," S-A, rounded corners, coil	$3	$2

Booklets		
(33c) Hat "H," S-A, die-cut 9.9, booklet	$1.20	$.20
(33c) Hat "H," S-A, die-cut 11 or 11-1/2, booklet	$1.30	$.20
(33c) Hat "H," S-A, die-cut 8, booklet	$1.20	$1

Coils	Unused	Used
(10c) Eagle & Shield "Presorted std" gummed	$.40	$.25
(10c) Eagle & Shield, self-adhesive	$.40	$.25

1999

	Unused	Used
33c Year of the Rabbit	$1.30	$.20
33c Malcolm X	$1.30	$.20
33c Love Valentine, cut to shape	$1.30	$.20
55c Love Valentine, cut to shape	$2	$.30
33c Hospice Care	$1.20	$.20

Regular Issues

	Unused	Used
33c Flag & City, perforated, red date	$1	$.30
33c Flag & City, S-A, black date, booklet	$1	$.30
33c Flag & City, S-A, red date, booklet	$1	$.30
33c Flag & City, perforated, coil	$	$.30
33c Flag & City, S-A, square corners, coil	$1	$.30
33c Flag & City, S-A, rounded corners, coil	$1	$.30
33c Flag & Chalkboard, S-A	$1.20	$.20

1999

	Unused	Used
33c Irish Immigration	$1.30	$.20
33c Alfred Lunt & Lynn Fontanne	$1.30	$.20

1999	Unused	Used
Arctic Animals, strip of 5	$7	---
33c Any single: Arctic Hare, Arctic Fox, Snowy Owl, Polar Bear, Gray Wolf	$1.20	$.30
Sonoran Desert, pane of 10	$12.50	---
33c Any single	$1	$.35
Berries, self-adhesive block of 4	$4	---
33c Any single: Blueberries, Raspberries, Strawberries, Blackberries, dated 1999 or 2000	$1	$.25
Berries, self-adhesive block of 4	$4	---
33c Any single: Blueberries, Strawberries, Raspberries, Blackberries	$1	$.25
Berries, self-adhesive, coil strip of 5	$4	---
33c Blueberry (2), Raspberry, Blackberry, Strawberry	$1	$.25
Daffy Duck, self-adhesive panes of 9 and 1	$12	---
33c Daffy Duck, die-cut single stamp, backing not cut	$1	$.25
33c Daffy Duck, single, without die-cut	$4	---
33c Ayn Rand	$1	$.20
33c Cinco de Mayo	$1	$.20
Tropical Flowers, integrated block of 4	$5	---
33c Any single: Bird of Paradise, Royal Poinciana, Gloriosa, Chinese Hibiscus	$1	$.30

1999	Unused	Used
33c John & William Bartram	$1	$.20
33c Prostate Cancer Awareness	$1	$.20
33c California Gold Rush	$2	$.20
Aquarium Fish strip of 4	$4	---
33c Any single: Yellow & Red Fish, Fish & Thermometer, Blue Fish, Hermit Crab	$1	$.20
Extreme Sports, block of 4	$4	---
33c Any single: Skateboarding, BMX Biking, Snowboarding, Inline Skating	$1	$.25
American Glass, block of 4	$4	---
33c Any single: Free-blown, Mold-blown, Pressed Glass, Art Glass	$1	$.25
33c James Cagney	$1.20	$.20

33c American Glass

32c Ballet

22c Uncle Sam, self-adhesive

33c Victorian Love, cut to shape

55c Victorian Love, cut to shape

33c Irish Immigration

Arctic Animals, strip of 5

1999	Unused	Used
55c Gen. Billy Mitchell	$2	$.50
33c Honoring Those Who Served	$1	$.25
45c Universal Postal Union	$1.50	$.25
Famous Trains, strip of 5	$5	---
33c Any single: Daylight, Congressional, 20th Century Limited, Hiawatha, Super Chief	$1	$.25
33c Frederick Law Olmsted	$1	$.30
Hollywood Composers, block of 6	$7	---
33c Any single: Max Steiner, Dimitri Tiomkin, Bernard Herrmann, Franz Waxman, Alfred Newman, Erich Wolfgang Korngold	$1	$.25
Broadway Songwriters, block of 6	$7	---
33c Any single: Ira & George Gershwin, Alan Jay Lerner & Frederick Loewe, Lorenz Hart, Richard Rodgers & Oscar Hammerstein II, Meredith Wilson, Frank Loesser	$1	$.25
Insects & Spiders, pane of 20	$20	---
33c Any single	$1	$.25
33c Hanukkah	$1	$.30
22c Uncle Sam Coil, perforation 9-3/4 vertically	$.60	$.25
33c NATO	$1	$.30
33c Christmas, Madonna & Child	$1	$.20
Christmas, Leaping Deer, S-A, cut 11-1/4, block of 4	$4	---

1999	Unused	Used
33c Any single: maroon, blue, purple, green	$1	$.20
Christmas, Leaping Deer, thicker frame line, pane of 4	$4	---
33c Any single: maroon, blue, purple, green	$1	$.20
33c Kwanzaa	$1	$.20
33c Year 2000, Baby New Year	$1	$.20

2000		
33c Year of the Dragon	$1	$.20
33c Patricia Roberts Harris	$1	$.20
33c Los Angeles Class Submarine, with micro-printed "USPS" at base of sail	$1	$.20
Submarine Prestige booklet, pane of 5	$20	---
22c S Class Submarine	$1	$.20
33c Los Angeles Class Submarine, no micro-printed "USPS"	$1	$.20
55c Ohio Class Submarine	$2	$.60
60c USS Holland	$2	$.60
$3.20 Gato Class Submarine	$5	$2.50
Pacific Coast Rain Forest, pane of 10	$10	---
Any single	$1	$.25
Louise Nevelson, strip of 5	$6	---

33c Daffy
Duck

33c Blackberry

33c California Gold Rush

*55c Gen.
Billy
Mitchell*

33c Los Angeles Class Submarine

33c Lt. Audie L. Murphy

$12.25 Washington Monument

Youth Team Sports

34c Yankee Stadium, New York City

34c Lucille Ball

34c Venus Flytrap

33c New Year 2000

2000	Unused	Used
Any single: Silent Music I, Royal Tide I, Black Chord, Nightsphere-Light, Dawn's Wedding Chapel I	$1.20	$.50
Hubble Space Telescope Images, strip of 5	$6	---
33c Any single: Eagle Nebula, Ring Nebula, Lagoon Nebula, Galaxy NGC 1316	$1.20	$.50
33c American Samoa	$1	$.20
33c Library of Congress	$1	$.20
Roadrunner & Wile E. Coyote, pane of 10	$12	---
33c Single stamp	$1.30	$.20
No die-cut on far right stamp	$20	---
Distinguished Soldiers, block of 4	$5	---
33c Maj. Gen. John L. Hines, Gen. Omar N. Bradley, Sgt. Alvin C. York, 2nd Lt. Audie L. Murphy	$1	$.20
33c Summer Sports, Runners	$1	$.20
33c Adoption	$1.20	$.20
Youth Team Sports, block of 4	$5	---
33c Any single: Basketball, Football, Soccer, Baseball	$1	$.20
Stars & Stripes, pane of 20 historical flags	$22	---
33c Any single	$1	$.50
Berries coils, die-cut 8-1/2 horizontally, strip of 5	$5	---
33c Any single: Blueberries (2), Strawberries, Blackberries, Raspberries	$1	$.20

33c White House

34c Flag Over Farm

2000	Unused	Used
Legends of Baseball, pane of 20	$20	---
33c Any single	$1	$.30
Probing the Vastness of Space, pane of 6	$15	---
60c Any single hologram	$1.20	$.75
Exploring the Solar System, pane of 5	$22	---
$1 Any single hologram	$2	$1.15
Escaping the Gravity of Earth, pane of 2	$25	---
$3.20 Any single hologram	$5	$2.20
Space Achievement & Exploration, pane of 1	$40	---
$11.75 Circular hologram stamp	$40	$10

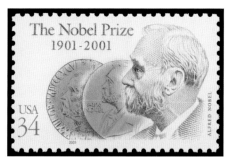

34c Nobel Prize

34c Porky Pig

34c Christmas Madonna & Child

2000	Unused	Used
Landing on the Moon, pane of 1	$40	---
$11.75 Single hologram stamp	$40	$10
33c California Statehood	$1.15	$.35
Stampin' the Future Children's Designs, strip of 4	$4	---
33c Any single: Crowded Space, Kids & Heart, "Mommy Are We There?" Dog in Space	$1	$.20
Distinguished Americans Definitive Series		
10c Gen. Joseph W. Stilwell	$.30	$.20
23c Wilma Rudolph	$1	$.50
23c Wilma Rudolph booklet single	$1	$.50
33c Sen. Claude Pepper	$1	$.75
58c Margaret Chase Smith	$1.25	$1
59c James Michener	$1.20	$1
76c Edward Trudeau	$1.60	$1.20
63c Jonas Salk	$2.25	$1
75c Harriet Beecher Stowe	$1.50	$1.25
76c Sen. Hattie Caraway	$2.50	$.60
78c Mary Lasker	$1.50	$1
83c Edna Ferber (2002)	$1.75	$.50
83c Edna Ferber (2003)	$3.25	$1.25
87c Albert Sabin	$3.50	$1.50

2000	Unused	Used
33c California Statehood	$1	$.20
Deep Sea Creatures, strip of 5	$6	---
33c Any single: Fanfin Anglerfish, Sea Cucumber, Fangtooth, Amphipod, Medusa	$1.20	$.25
33c Thomas Wolfe	$1	$.30
33c White House	$1.50	$.30
33c Edward G. Robinson	$3.15	$.70
2000 Regular Issues		
(10c) N.Y. Public Library Lion, S-A coil	$.50	$.25
(34c) Flag Over Farm, perforation 11-1/4	$1.15	$.45
(34c) Flag Over Farm, die-cut 11-1/4	$1.20	$.25
(34c) Flag Over Farm, booklet, die-cut 8	$1.15	$.30
(34c) Statue of Liberty, horizontal self-adhesive booklet	$1.15	$.20
(34c) Statue of Liberty, coil, perforation 9-3/4 vertically	$1.15	$.20
(34c) Statue of Liberty, S-A coil, cut 10 vertically	$1.15	$.20
Flowers, S-A booklet, die-cut 10-1/4 x 10-3/4 block of 4	$4	---
(34c) Any single: Purple, Tan, Green, Red	$1	$.20
Flowers, S-A booklet, die-cut 11-1/2 x 11-3/4 block of 4	$4	---
(34c) Any single: Purple, Tan, Green, Red	$1	$.20

2000 Regular Issues	Unused	Used
Flowers, S-A coil, die-cut 8-1/2 vertically, strip of 5	$5	---
(34c) Any single: Green (2), Red, Tan, Purple	$1	$.20
2001		
34c Statue of Liberty, S-A coil, die-cut 9-3/4 vertically, rounded corners	$1.15	$.30
21c Buffalo (gummed)	$.80	$.50
21c Buffalo (self-adhesive)	$.80	$.30
23c Washington (self-adhesive)	$.85	$.50
34c Flag Over Farm (gummed)	$1.25	$.80
34c Flag Over Farm (die-cut 11-1/4)	$1.25	$.60
55c Art Deco Eagle (die-cut 10-3/4)	$2	$.50
57c Art Deco Eagle	$2	$.50
$3.50 Capitol Dome	$12.50	$4
$12.25 Washington Monument	$30	$8
21c Buffalo, self-adhesive, coil, cut 8-1/2 vertically	$.85	$.30
23c Washington, green, self-adhesive coil	$.85	$.30
34c Statue of Liberty, coil, perforated, 9-3/4	$1	$.25
34c Statue of Liberty, self adhesive, cut 9-3/4, square corners	$1	$.25

2001	Unused	Used
Flowers, S-A coil, die-cut 8-1/2 vertically, strip of 5	$5	---
34c Any single: Green (2), Red, Tan, Purple	$1	$.20
20c Washington, dark carmine booklet S-A, cut 11-1/2	$.80	$.20
20c Washington, dark carmine booklet S-A, die-cut 10-1/2 x 11-1/2	$.80	$.25
21c Bison self-adhesive die-cut 11-1/2 booklet	$.80	$.25
21c Bison self-adhesive die-cut 10-1/2 x 11-1/2 booklet	$2	$.25
34c Statue of Liberty, self-adhesive, cut 11	$1	$.25
Flowers, self-adhesive booklet block of 4, cut 10-1/4 x 10-3/4	$4	---
34c Any single: Purple, Tan, Green, Red	$1	$.25
Apple & Orange S-A booklet, cut 11-1/2 x 10-3/4 pair	$2	
34c Either single: Apple or Orange	$1	$.25
Apple & Orange S-A booklet, cut 11-1/4, pair	$2	---
34c Either single: Apple or Orange	$1	$.25
34c Flag Over Farm, S-A booklet, die-cut 8	$1	$.25
(34c) Love, Letter & Rose, self-adhesive booklet	$1	$.25
34c Love, Letter & Rose, self-adhesive booklet, 19-1/2 x 26-1/2 mm, die-cut 11-1/4	$1	$.25

2001	Unused	Used
34c Love, Letter & Rose, self-adhesive booklet, 18 x 21 mm, die-cut 11-1/2 x 10-3/4	$1	$.25
55c Love, Letter & Rose, self-adhesive booklet	$2	$.50
34c Year of the Snake	$1.20	$.25
34c Roy Wilkins	$1	$.25
American Illustrators, pane of 20	$25	---
34c Any single	$1	$.25
34c Diabetes	$1	$.25
34c Nobel Prize	$1	$.25
Pan American Inverts centennial souvenir sheet of 7	$12	---
1c Ship Inverted	$.60	$.40
2c Train Inverted	$.60	$.40
4c Automobile Inverted	$.60	$.40
80c Expo Seal	$4	$2
Great Plains Prairie, pane of 10	$12	---
34c Any single stamp	$1.20	$.30
34c Peanuts—Snoopy	$2	$.25
34c Honoring Veterans	$1.20	$.20
34c Frida Kahlo	$1	$.20
Legendary Baseball Playing Fields, block of 10	$12	---

2001	Unused	Used
34c Any single	$1	$.25
(10c) Atlas, self-adhesive coil, cut 8-1/2	$.50	$.20
34c Leonard Bernstein	$1.20	$.30
(15c) "Woody" Wagon, self-adhesive coil, cut 11-1/2	$.60	$.35
34c Lucille Ball	$1.50	$.30
Amish Quilts, block of 4	$5	---
34c Any single: Diamond in Square, Starburst, Diamond, Double Ninepatch	$1.20	$.40
Carnivorous Plants, block or strip of 4	$5	---
34c Any single: Venus Flytrap, Yellow Trumpet, Cobra Lily, English Sundew	$1.20	$.25
34c Eid Mubarek	$1.20	$.30
34c Enrico Fermi	$1.20	$.20
Porky Pig, pane of 10	$12	---
34c single stamp	$1.20	$.20
Pane of 1 without die-cuts	$20	---
34c Christmas, Madonna & Child	$1.20	$.20
Christmas, Santa Clauses, strip of 4	$5	---
34c Any single: Santa with horse, with horn, with red hat, with dog, black inscription	$1.20	$.20
Christmas, Santa Clauses, booklet	$5	---

2001	Unused	Used
34c Any single: Santas as above, red & green inscription and smaller year date	$1.20	$.20
34c James Madison	$1.20	$.20
34c We Give Thanks	$1.20	$.20
34c Hanukkah	$1.20	$.20
34c Kwanzaa	$1.20	$.20
34c United We Stand booklet, 2001 year date	$1.20	$.20
34c United We Stand booklet, 2002 year date	$1.20	$.20
34c United We Stand, coil, square corners	$1.20	$.20
34c United We Stand, coil, rounded corners	$1.30	$.70
57c Love, Letter & Rose	$2	$.80

2002		
Winter Sports, strip of 4	$5	---
34c Any single: Ski Jumping, Snowboarding, Ice Hockey, Figure Skating	$1.20	$.30
34c Mentoring a Child	$1.20	$.20
34c Langston Hughes	$1.40	$.20
34c Happy Birthday	$1.40	$.20
34c Year of the Horse	$1.30	$.20
34c West Point	$1.30	$.20
Greetings From America, pane of 50	$55	---

37c
Irving
Berlin

37c
Louisiana
Purchase

34c Love Letters

1c Tiffany Lamp

2002	Unused	Used
34c Any single	$1.20	$.25
Pine Forest, pane of 10	$12	---
34c Any single	$1.20	$.25
5c American Toleware, Coffee Pot, coil	$.30	$.20
3c Red, White & Blue Star, date on left	$.20	$.20
3c Red, White & Blue Star, date on right	$.20	$.20
3c Red, White & Blue Star, coil	$.20	$.20
23c George Washington, green, 2002 date	$1	$.25
23c Washington, green, coil, 2002 date	$1	$.25
23c Washington, green, booklet	$1	$.25
(37c) Waving Flag, perforation 11-1/4 x 11	$1	$.25
(37c) Flag, self-adhesive, microprinting "USA"	$1	$.25
(37c) Flag, coil, self-adhesive	$1	$.25
(37c) Flag, booklet, microprinting "USPS"	$2.50	$.25
(37c) Flag, booklet, large "2002," cut 10-1/2 x 10-3/4	$1	$.25
(37c) Flag, booklet, large "2002," cut 8	$1	$.25
Antique Toys booklet, block of 4	$4	---
(37c) Any single: Mail Wagon, Locomotive, Taxicab, Fire Engine	$1	$.25
37c Waving Flag, perforation 11-1/4, date 2003	$1	$.25

2002	Unused	Used
37c Flag, microprinting "USA," 2002 date	$1	$.25
37c Flag, coil, perforation 10	$1	$.25
37c Flag, coil, self-adhesive, cut 9-3/4, 2002 date	$1	$.25
37c Flag, coil, S-A, cut 10-1/5, 2003 date	$1	$.25
37c Flag, coil, S-A, cut 8-1/2, 2002 date	$1	$.25
37c Flag, coil, S-A, cut 8-1/2, 2003 date	$3	$.25
37c Flag, coil, microprinting "USA,"2005	$3	$.25
37c Flag, coil, S-A, cut 11-3/4, 2004 date	$1	$.25
37c Flag, booklet, S-A, cut 10-1/2 x 10-3/4	$1	$.25
37c Flag, booklet, S-A, cut 11-1/4 x 11, 2004 date	$1	$.25
37c Flag, booklet, S-A cut 11	$1	$.25
37c Flag, booklet, S-A, cut 8, 2003 date	$1	$.25
Antique Toys, self-adhesive coil, strip of 4	$5	---
37c Any single: Fire Engine, Taxicab, Locomotive, Mail Wagon	$1	$.25
Antique Toys, self-adhesive booklet, block of 4	$5	---
37c Any single: Mail Wagon, Locomotive, Taxicab, Fire Engine	$1	$.25
60c Eagle Coverlet	$2	$.30
$3.85 Jefferson Memorial, 2002 date	$10	$5
$3.85 Jefferson Memorial, 2003 date	$10	$5

2002	Unused	Used
$13.65 Capitol Dome	$32	$8
American Photography, pane of 20	$25	---
37c Any single	$1.20	$.75
37c John James Audubon	$2	$.20
37c Harry Houdini	$1.50	$.20
37c Andy Warhol	$1.20	$.20
Teddy Bears, block of 4	$8	---
37c Any single: Bruin, Stick, Gund, Ideal	$2	$.25
34c Love	$1.50	$.25
60c Love	$2.30	$.50
37c Ogden Nash	$1.30	$.20
37c Duke Kahanamoku	$1.25	$.20
American Bats, strip of 4	$7	---
37c Any single: Red, Leaf-Nosed, Pallid, Spotted	$1.20	$.25
Women Journalists, block of 4	$6	---
37c Any single: Nellie Bly, Ida M. Tarbell, Ethel L. Payne, Marguerite Higgins	$1.30	$.50
37c Irving Berlin	$1.30	$.20
Neuter & Spay, pair	$2	---
37c Any single: Cat or Dog	$1	$.20
37c Hanukkah	$1.20	$.20

2002	Unused	Used
37c Kwanzaa	$1.20	$.20
37c Eid	$1.20	$.25
37c Christmas, Madonna & Child	$1.20	$.20
Snowmen, strip of 4	$5	---
37c Any single: Red plaid scarf, Blue plaid, Cork pipe, Top hat	$1.20	$.20
Snowmen, coil, strip of 4, smaller format	$5	---
37c Any single: Blue plaid, Cork pipe, Top hat, Red plaid	$1.20	$.20
	$5	---
37c Any single: Red plaid, Blue plaid, Cork pipe, Top hat	$1.20	$.20
Snowmen, booklet, self-adhesive, die-cut 11	$5	---
37c Any single: Red plaid, Blue plaid, Cork pipe, Top hat	$1.20	$.20
37c Cary Grant	$1.30	$.40
5c Sea Coast	$.20	$.20
Hawaiian Missionary Stamps, souvenir sheet of 4	$5	---
37c Any single	$1.25	$.30
37c Happy Birthday	$1.30	$.20
Greetings From America, pane of 50	$55	---
37c Any single	$1	$.50

2003	Unused	Used
37c Thurgood Marshall	$1.20	$.20
37c Year of the Ram	$1	$.20
37c Zora Neale Hurston	$1	$.20
American Design Series		
1c Tiffany Lamp	$.20	$.20
2c Navajo Necklace, any version	$.20	$.20
3c Silver Coffeepot	$.20	$.20
4c Chippendale Chair	$.20	$.20
5c Toleware Coffeepot	$.20	$.20
5c Toleware Coffeepot, 2007	$.20	$.20
10c American Clock	$.20	$.20
1c Tiffany Lamp, coil	$.20	$.20
3c Silver Coffeepot, coil	$.20	$.20
4c Chippendale Chair, coil	$.20	$.20
10c American Clock, coil	$.20	$.20
American Culture Series		
$1 Wisdom	$2	$.50
10c N.Y. Public Library Lion, coil, date 2003	$.30	$.20
10c Atlas Statue, S-A, cut 11, date 2003	$.30	$.20

37c American Filmmakers sheetlet

American Culture Series	Unused	Used
80c Special Olympics	$2	$1
American Filmmaking, pane of 10	$15	---
37c Any single	$1.20	$.30
37c Ohio Statehood	$1.30	$.20
37c Pelican Island	$1.30	$.20
5c Seacoast, coil, blue 2003	$.20	$.25
5c Seacoast, die-cut 4 sides, black 2003	$.20	$.20
Old Glory, presentation booklet of 20 stamps	$25	---
37c Any single: Uncle Sam on Bicycle, Campaign Badge, Bookmark, Flag on Fan, Liberty Figure	$1.50	$1
37c Cesar Chavez	$1.20	$.20
37c Louisiana Purchase	$1.20	$.20
37c First Flight Centennial	$1.20	$.20
37c Purple Heart, die-cut 11-1/4 x 10-3/4	$1.20	$.30
37c Purple Heart, die-cut 10-3/4 x 10-1/4	$1.20	$.30
37c Audrey Hepburn	$1.50	$.20

2003		
Southeastern Lighthouses, strip of 5	$7.50	---
37c Any single: Cape Henry, Cape Lookout, Morris Island, Tybee Island, Hillsboro Inlet	$1.20	$.40

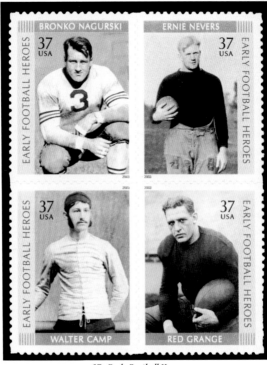

37c Early Football Heroes

2003	Unused	Used
2003 Eagle & Shield Coil, die-cut 11-3/4, strip of 10	$10	---
25c Any single: Gold on gray, Red on gold, Gold on dull blue, Prussian blue on gold, Gold on green, Gray on gold, Gold on Prussian blue, Dull blue on gold, Gold on red, Green on gold	$.80	$.50
Arctic Tundra, pane of 10	$12	---
37c Any single	$1.20	$.50
37c Korean War Veterans Memorial	$1.20	$.20
Mary Cassatt, block of 4	$5	---
37c Any single: Young Mother, Playing on the Beach, On a Balcony, Child in a Straw Hat	$1.20	$.30
Early Football Heroes, block of 4	$5	---
37c Any single: Bronko Nagurski, Ernie Nevers, Walter Camp, Red Grange	$1.20	$.30
37c Roy Acuff	$1.20	$.25
37c District of Columbia	$1.30	$.30
Reptiles & Amphibians, strip of 5	$6	---
37c Any single: Scarlet king snake, Blue-spotted salamander, Reticulate collared lizard, Ornate chorus frog, Ornate box turtle	$1.20	$.30
23c Washington, green, die-cut 11	$.60	$.50
37c Christmas, Madonna & Child	$1.20	$.30
Christmas, Holiday Music Makers, strip of 4	$5	---

37c Reptiles and Amphibians

37c World War II Memorial

37c John Wayne

2003	Unused	Used
37c Any single: Deer with pipes, Santa with drum, Santa with horn, Deer with horn	$1.20	$.30
Christmas, Holdiay Music Makers booklet, strip of 4	$5	---
37c Any single: Deer with pipes, Santa with drum, Santa with horn, Deer with horn	$1.20	$.30
37c Snowy Egret, coil, date 2003	$1.20	$.25
37c Snowy Egret, coil, date 2004	$1.20	$.20
37c Snowy Egret, booklet	$1.20	$.20
2004		
Pacific Coral Reef, pane of 10	$12	---
37c Any single	$1.20	$.35
37c Year of the Monkey	$1.20	$.20
37c Love, Candy Hearts	$1.20	$.20
37c Paul Robeson	$1.30	$.20
37c Dr. Seuss	$1.20	$.20
37c Garden Bouquet	$1.20	$.20
60c Garden Bouquet	$2	$.30
37c U.S. Air Force Academy	$1.20	$.20
37c Henry Mancini	$1.20	$.20
American Choreographers, block of 4	$5	---

2004	Unused	Used
37c Any single: Martha Graham, Alvin Ailey, Agnes de Mille, George Ballanchine	$1.20	$.30
2004 Definitive Eagle & Shield Coil, perforation 9.9, strip of 10	$10	---
25c Any single: Gold on gray, Green on gold, Gold on red, Dull blue on gold, Gold on Prussian blue, Gray on gold, Gold on green, Prussian blue on gold, Gold on dull blue, Red on gold	$.90	$.70
37c Lewis & Clark Bicentennial, booklet of 20	$25	---
37c Any single: Lewis & Clark at Outlook, Merriweather Lewis, William Clark	$1.20	$.30
Isamu Noguchi, strip of 5	$6	---
37c Any single: Akari, Maret LaFarge Osborn, Black Sun, Mother & Child, Figure	$1.20	$.30
37c World War II Memorial	$1.20	$.20
37c Summer Olympic Games	$1.20	$.20
5c Sea Coast, black 2004	$.20	$.20
5c Sea Coast, black 2003, die-cut 10	$.20	$.20
5c Sea Coast, black 2004, die-cut 11-1/5	$.20	$.20
The Art of Disney, block of 4	$5	---
37c Any single: Goofy, Mickey & Donald; Bambi & Thumper; Mufasa & Simba; Jiminy Cricket & Pinocchio	$1.20	$.30

2004	Unused	Used
37c USS Constellation	$1.60	$.20
37c R. Buckminster Fuller	$1.20	$.20
37c James Baldwin	$1.20	$.20
37c Martin Johnson Heade	$1.20	$.30
Art of the American Indian, pane of 10	$15	---
37c Any single	$1.20	$.20
37c John Wayne	$1.50	$.30
37c Sickle Cell Awareness	$1.30	$.30
Cloudscapes, pane of 15	$22	---
37c Any single	$1.20	$.20
37c Christmas, Madonna & Child	$1.20	$.20
37c Hanukkah	$1.20	$.20
37c Kwanzaa	$1.20	$.20
37c Moss Hart	$1.20	$.20
Christmas Santa Ornaments, strip of 4	$5	---
37c Any single: Purple, Green, Blue, Red	$1.20	$.20
Christmas, Santa Ornaments, booklet, cut 10-1/4 x 10-3/4	$5	---

2004	Unused	Used
37c Any single: Purple, Green, Blue, Red	$1.20	$.20
Christmas, Santa Ornaments, booklet, die-cut 8	$5	---
37c Any single: Green, Purple, Red, Blue	$1.20	$.20

2005		
Lunar New Year, pane of 12	$18	---
37c Any single	$1.20	$.20
37c Marian Anderson	$1.20	$.20
37c Ronald Reagan	$1.20	$.20
37c Love Bouquet	$1.20	$.20
Northeast Deciduous Forest, pane of 10	$12	---
37c Any single	$1.20	$.25
Spring Flowers booklet, strip of 4	$5	---
37c Any single: Hyacinth, Daffodil, Tulip, Iris	$1.20	$.20
37c Robert Penn Warren	$1.20	$.20
37c "Yip" Harburg	$1.20	$.20
American Scientists, block of 4	$5	---
37c Any single: Barbara McClintock, Josiah Willard Gibbs, John von Neumann, Richard Feynman	$1.20	$.30
Modern American Architecture, pane of 12	$15	---
37c Any single	$1.20	$.40

2005	Unused	Used
37c Henry Fonda	$1.30	$.25
The Art of Disney, block of 4	$5	$.20
37c Any single: Mickey & Pluto, Mad Hatter and Alice, Ariel & Flounder, Snow White & Dopey	$1.20	$.20
American Advances in Aviation, block of 10	$12	---
37c Any single	$1.20	$.20
New Mexico Rio Grande Blankets, block of 4	$5	---
37c Any single	$1.20	$.20
37c Presidential Libraries	$1.20	$.20
America on the Move, strip of 5	$7	---
37c Any single; Studebaker Starliner, Kaiser Darrin, Chevrolet Corvette, Nash Healey, Ford Thunderbird	$1.40	$.30
37c Arthur Ashe	$1.20	$.20
To Form a More Perfect Union, pane of 10	$12	---
37c Any single	$1.20	$.20
37c Child Health	$1.20	$.20
Let's Dance, block of 4	$5	---
37c Any single: Merengue, Salsa, Cha Cha, Mambo	$1.20	$.20
37c Greta Garbo	$1.20	$.20
Jim Henson & the Muppets, pane of 11	$15	---

37c Cloudscapes sheetlet

37c Christmas Madonna & Child

37c Robert Penn Warren

2005	Unused	Used
37c Any single	$1.20	$.20
Constellations, strip of 4	$5	---
37c Any single: Leo, Orion, Lyra, Pegasus	$1.20	$.20
Christmas, Cookies, strip of 4	$5	---
37c Any single: Santa, Snowmen, Angel, Elves	$1.20	$.20
Christmas, Cookies, booklet, strip of 4	$5	$.20
37c Any single: Santa, Snowmen, Angel, Elves	$1.20	$.20
Christmas, Cookies, booklet, smaller format	$5	---
37c Any single: Santa, Snowmen, Angel, Elves	$1.30	$.20
Distinguished Marines, block of 4	$5	---
37c Any single: John W. Lejeune, Lewis B. "Chesty" Puller, John Basilone, Daniel Daly	$1.20	$.20
2005-06 Definitives, Statue of Liberty & Flag, non-denominated "First Class"		
(39c) Liberty & Flag, perforation 11-1/4	$1.50	$.20
(39c) Liberty & Flag, cut 11-1/4 x 10-3/4, micro USPS	$1.50	$.20
(39c) Liberty & Flag, coil, perforation 9-3/4	$1.50	$.20
(39c) Liberty & Flag, coil, small date, cut 8-1/2	$1	$.20
(39c) Liberty & Flag, coil, large date, cut 10-1/4	$1.50	$.20
(39c) Liberty & Flag, coil, micro USPS, cut 9-1/2	$1.50	$.20
(39c) Liberty & Flag, booklet, cut 11-1/4 x 10-3/4	$1.50	$.20

37c The Art of Disney

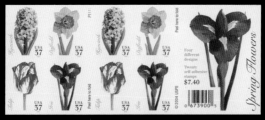

Spring Flowers booklet

2005-06 Definitives, Statue of Liberty & Flag, non-denominated "First Class"	Unused	Used
(39c) Liberty & Flag, booklet, large date	$1.50	$.20
(39c) Liberty & Flag, booklet, small blue date	$1.50	$.20
(39c) Liberty & Flag, booklet, die-cut 8	$1.50	$.20
(39c) Love, True Blue Birds, booklet	$1.20	$.20
2006 Definitives, Statue Liberty & Flag, denominated "39"		
39c Liberty & Flag, microprinting USPS	$1.50	$.20
39c Liberty & Flag, coil, perforation 10	$1.50	$.20
39c Liberty & Flag, coil, die-cut 11	$1.50	$.20
39c Liberty & Flag, coil, cut 9-1/2, micro USPS	$1.50	$.20

37c Jim Henson (and Muppets) sheetlet

39c Olympic Winter Games

39c Katherine Anne Porter

39c Amber Alert

2006 Definitives, Statue Liberty & Flag, denominated "39"	Unused	Used
39c Liberty & Flag, coil, die-cut 10-1/4	$1.50	$.20
39c Liberty & Flag, coil, die-cut 8-1/2	$1.50	$.20
39c Liberty & Flag, booklet, die-cut 11-1/4 x 10-3/4	$1.50	$.20

2006	Unused	Used
Favorite Children's Book Animals, block of 8	$10	---
39c Any single	$1.20	$.20
39c Winter Olympics, downhill skiing	$1.20	$.20
39c Hattie McDaniel	$1.20	$.20
Lunar New Year, pane of 12	$15	---
39c Any single	$1.20	$.20
39c Purple Dove	$1.20	$.20
63c Green Dove	$2	$.50
24c Common Buckeye Butterfly, perforation 11-1/4	$1	$.20
24c Common Buckeye, self-adhesive, die-cut 11	$1	$.20
24c Common Buckeye, coil	$1	$.20
Crops of the Americas, strip of 5	$6	---
39c Any single: Peppers, Beans, Sunflower, Squash, Corn	$1.50	$.30
Crops of the Americas, convertible booklet cut 10-3/4 x 10-1/2	$6	---
39c Any single: Corn, Squash, Sunflower, Beans, Peppers	$1.50	$.30
Crops of the Americas, vending booklet cut 10-3/4 x 11-1/4	$6	---
39c Any single: Pepper, Corn, Squash, Sunflower, Beans	$1.60	$.60
$4.05 X Plane Priority Mail	$8	$6

2006	Unused	Used
$14.40 X Plane Express Mail	$29	$10
39c Sugar Ray Robinson	$1.50	$.30
Benjamin Franklin, block of 4	$5	---
39c Any single: Statesman, Scientist, Printer, Postmaster	$1.60	$.30
The Art of Disney -- Romance, block of 4	$6	---
39c Any single: Mickey & Minnie, Beauty & the Beast, Cinderella & Prince Charming, Lady & the Tramp	$1.40	$.40
39c Love, True Blue booklet	$1.20	$.20
39c Katherine Anne Porter	$1.20	$.20
39c Amber Alert	$1.20	$.20
39c Purple Heart	$1.20	$.20
Wonders of America, pane of 40	$48	---
39c Any single	$1.20	$.40
39c Samuel de Champlain	$1.40	$.30
The 1606 Voyage of Champlain, souvenir sheet of 4, with Canada and U.S. stamps	$6	---
Washington 2006 Philatelic Exhibition, souvenir sheet	$30	---
$1 Memorial from 1922-25 issue	$5	---
$2 Capitol	$10	---

Washington 2006 World Philatelic Exhibition souvenir sheet

2006	Unused	Used
$5 America statue	$15	---
Distinguished American Diplomats, block of 6	$7	---
39c Any single	$1.20	$.20
39c Judy Garland	$1.50	$.40

2006	Unused	Used
39c Ronald Reagan	$1.50	$.20
39c Happy Birthday	$1.30	$.30
Baseball Sluggers, block of 4	$5	---
39c Any single: Roy Campanella, Hank Greenberg, Mel Ott, Mickey Mantle	$1.30	$.30
DC Comics Superheroes, pane of 20	$28	---
39c Any single	$1.50	$.30
American Motorcycles, strip of 4	$5	---
39c Any single: Indian, Cleveland, Chopper, Harley-Davidson	$1.50	$.30
Quilts of Gee's Bend, block of 10	$15	---
39c Any single	$1.40	$.30
Southern Florida Wetlands, pane of 10	$15	---
39c Any single	$1.20	$.30
39c Christmas, Madonna & Child	$1.20	$.20
Christmas, Snowflakes, 2006 lower than USA, strip of 4	$6	---
39c Any single	$1.60	$.30
Christmas, Snowflakes, booklet, cut 11-1/4 x 11-1/2	$7	---
39c Any single	$1.80	$.60
Christmas, Snowflakes, booklet, cut 11-1/4 x 11	$10	---
39c Any single	$2	$.70
Christmas, Snowflakes, booklet, die-cut 8	$7	---

39c DC Comics Super Heroes

2006	Unused	Used
39c Any single	$1.60	$.60
39c Eid	$1.30	$.20
39c Hanukkah	$1.30	$.20
39c Kwanzaa	$1.30	$.20
2007		
39c Ella Fitzgerald	$1.30	$.20
39c Oklahoma Statehood	$1.30	$.20
39c With Love and Kisses	$1.30	$.20
$1.68 International Polar Year, souvenir sheet of 2	$3	---
39c Henry Wadsworth Longfellow	$1.30	$.20

39c Christmas, Madonna & Child   *41c Darth Vader – Star Wars*

84c International Polar Year sheetlet

'FOREVER' STAMPS

The idea of a stamp that always would remain valid for the mailing of a letter, despite rate increases, is as revolutionary as the original idea of pre-paid postage more than 150 years ago.

People who bought a supply of 41-cent Liberty Bell "forever" stamps in 2007 could still use them after the first-class mail rate increased to 44 cents in 2009 – for a paper profit of 7% -- and the stamps would remain valid through future rate hikes.

The Postal Service also offered "forever" Evergreen stamps as part of its Christmas offerings in 2010 and announced that others would follow.

26c Florida Panther,
self-adhesive, coil

42c American Journalists, strip of 5

Tropical Fruit, coil

2007	Unused	Used
(41c) Liberty Bell, large micro Forever, bell 16 mm	$.80	$.20
(41c) Liberty Bell, small micro Forever, bell 16 mm	$.80	$.20
(41c) Liberty Bell, med micro Forever, bell 15 mm	$.80	$.20
(41c) Liberty Bell, ATM booklet	$.80	$.20
(41c) Flag, perforation	$.80	$.20

2007	Unused	Used
(41c) Flag, self-adhesive, microprinting USPS	$.80	$.20
(41c) Flag, coil, perforation, microprinting USPS	$.80	$.20
(41c) Flag, coil, die-cut 9-1/2, micro USPS	$.80	$.20
(41c) Flag, coil, die-cut 11	$.80	$.20
(41c) Flag, coil, die-cut 8-1/2	$.80	$.20
(41c) Flag, coil, die-cut 11, rounded corners	$.80	$.20
Jamestown Settlement, souvenir sheetlet of 20	$35	---
41c Jamestown triangle stamp	$1.40	$.30
2007 Definitives		
26c Florida Panther, perforated, micro USPS	$.50	$.30
26c Florida Panther, self-adhesive, micro USPS	$.50	$.30
26c Florida Panther, self-adhesive, coil	$.50	$.30
26c Florida Panther, booklet	$.50	$.30
17c Big Horn Sheep, self-adhesive	$.35	$.20
17c Big Horn Sheep, coil	$.35	$.20
Star Wars, pane of 15	$.20	---
41c Any single	$1	$.30

2007	Unused	Used
$4.60 Air Force One Priority Mail	$12	$6
$16.25 Marine One Express Mail	$40	$20
Pacific Lighthouses, strip of 5	$6	---
41c Any single: Diamond Head, Five Finger, Grays Harbor, Umpqua River, St. George Reef	$1	$.40
41c Hearts, lavender	$1	$.20
58c Hearts, pink	$1.50	$.40
Pollination, integrated block of 4	$5	---
41c Any single: Bee, Hummingbird, Bat, Butterfly	$1	$.30

2007 Definitives		
(10c) Patriotic Banner, S-A, rounded corners	$.20	$.20
(10c) Patriotic Banner, S-A, pointed corners	$.20	$.20
Marvel Comics, pane of 20	$25	---
41c Any single	$1	$.30
Vintage Mahogany Speedboats, strip of 4	$5	---
41c Any single: Hutchinson, Chris-Craft, Hacker-Craft, Gar Wood	$1	$.25
41c Purple Heart	$1	$.30
41c Louis Comfort Tiffany	$1	$.20

2007	Unused	Used
Flowers coils, strip of 10	$10	---
41c Any single: Iris, Dahlia, Magnolia, Red Gerbera Daisy, Coneflower, Tulip, Water Lily, Poppy, Chrysanthemum, Orange Gerbera Daisy	$1	$.30
Flowers booklet, block of 10	$10	---
41c Any single: Chrysanthemum, Orange Gerbera Daisy, Iris, Dahlia, Magnolia, Red Gerbera Daisy, Water Lily, Poppy, Coneflower, Tulip	$1	$.30
41c American Flag, denominated 41, coil, cut 8-1/2	$.85	$.20
41c Flag, coil, die-cut 11	$.85	$.20
41c Flag, coil, die-cut 9-1/2	$.85	$.20
41c Flag, coil	$.85	$.20
41c Flag, booklet, light gray flagpole	$.85	$.20
41c Flag, booklet, dark gray flagpole	$.85	$.20
The Art of Disney – Magic, block of 4	$5	---
41c Any single: Mickey Mouse, Tinkerbell & Peter Pan, Dumbo & Timothy Mouse, Aladdin & Genie	$1	$.25
41c Celebrate!	$1	$.20
41c James Stewart	$1	$.30
Alpine Tundra, pane of 10	$12	---
41c Any single	$1	$.20

2007	Unused	Used
41c Gerald R. Ford	$1	$.25
41c Jury Duty	$1	$.20
41c Mendez vs. Westminster School District	$1	$.25
41c Eid	$1	$.20
Polar Lights, pane of 2	$2	---
41c Any single: Aurora Borealis, Aurora Australis	$1	$.35
41c Yoda	$1.20	$.30
41c Christmas, Madonna & Child	$1	$.20
Christmas, Knit Designs, block of 4	$5	---
41c Any single: Reindeer, Tree, Snowman, Bear	$1	$.20
Christmas Knit Designs, small size, block of 4	$5	---
41c Any single	$1	$.20
Christmas, Knit Designs, ATM booklet, block of 4	$5	---
41c Any single	$1	$.20
41c Hanukkah	$1	$.20
41c Kwanzaa	$1	$.20
2008		
41c Year of the Rat	$1	$.20
41c Charles W. Chesnutt	$1	$.20
41c Marjorie Kinnan Rawlings	$1	$.20

2008	Unused	Used
American Scientists, block of 4	$5	---
41c Any single: Gerty Cori, Linus Pauling, Edwin Hubble, John Bardeen	$1	$.20
1c Tiffany Lamp, American Design Series	$.20	$.20
American Flag Scenes coils, perforated, strip of 4	$5	---
42c Any single: Dusk, Night, Dawn, Midday	$1	$.20
American Flag coils, die-cut 9-1/2	$5	---
42c Any single: Dusk, Night, Dawn, Midday	$1	$.20
American Flag coils, die-cut 11	$5	---
42c Any single: Dusk, Night, Dawn, Midday	$1	$.20
American Flag coils, die-cut 8-1/2	$5	---
42c Any single: Dusk, Night, Dawn, Midday	$1	$.20
American Flag coils, die-cut 11, rounded corners	$5	---
42c Any single: Dusk, Night, Dawn, Midday	$1	$.20
American Journalists, strip of 5	$6	---
42c Any single: Martha Gelhorn, John Hersey, George Polk, Ruben Salazar, Eric Sevareid	$1.20	$.20
Tropical Fruit, strip of 5, cut 11-1/4 x 10-3/4	$5	---
42c Any single: Pomegranate, Star Fruit, Kiwi, Papaya, Guava	$.85	$.20
Tropical Fruit, coil, strip of 5, cut 8-1/2	$5	---

2008	Unused	Used
42c Any single: Pomegranate, Star Fruit, Kiwi, Papaya, Guava	$.85	$.20
42c Purple Heart, perforated	$1	$.20
42c Purple Heart, self-adhesive	$1	$.20
42c Frank Sinatra	$1.20	$.30
42c Minnesota Statehood	$1	$.20
62c Dragonfly	$1.15	$.40
$4.80 Mt. Rushmore Priority	$10	$4
$16.50 Hoover Dam Express Mail	$38	$20
1c Tiffany Lamp, coil	$.20	$.20
10c American Clock, coil, perforated	$.20	$.20
42c Oversize Heart	$1	$.20
42c Filigree Heart	$1	$.20
59c Filigree Heart	$1.15	$.40
Flags of Our Nation, coil strip of 10	$15	---
42c Any single: American Flag, Alabama, Alaska, American Samoa, Arizona, Arkansas, California, Colorado, Connecticut, Delaware	$1	$.35
Charles & Ray Eames, Designers, pane of 16	$20	---
42c Any single	$1	$.40
42c Summer Olympics	$1	$.20
42c Celebrate!	$1	$.25

2008	Unused	Used
Vintage Black Cinema, strip of 5	$6	---
42c Any single: Black and Tan, The Sport of the Gods, Princess Tam-Tam, Caldonia, Hallelujah	$1	$.30
42c Take Me Out to the Ball Game	$1	$.25
The Art of Disney – Imagination, block of 4	$5	---
42c Any single: Lucky & Pongo, Mickey Mouse, Sleeping Beauty, Mowgli & Baloo	$1	$.25
42c Albert Bierstadt	$1	$.20
42c Sunflower	$1	$.20
5c American Toleware	$.20	$.20
Flags of Our Nation, coil strip of 10	$15	---
42c Any single: District of Columbia, Florida, Georgia, Guam, Hawaii, Idaho, Illinois, Indiana, Iowa, Kansas	$1	$.20
(5c) Seacoast, coil, perforated	$.20	$.20
$1 Wisdom, 2008 date	$2	$.50
42c Latin Jazz	$1	$.20
42c Bette Davis	$1	$.30
42c Eid	$1	$.20
Great Lakes Dunes, pane of 10	$12	---
42c Any single	$1	$.25
Tail Fins & Chrome, strip of 5	$6	---

2008	Unused	Used
42c Any single: Chrysler 300C, Lincoln Premier, Pontiac Safari, Studebaker Golden Hawk, Cadillac Eldorado	$1	$.30
42c Alzheimer's Awareness	$1	$.25
Christmas, Nutcrackers, strip of 4 from pane of 20	$5	---
42c Any single: Drummer, Santa, King, Soldier	$1	$.20
Christmas, Nutcrackers, strip of 4, booklet	$5	---
42c Any single: Drummer, Santa, King, Soldier	$1	$.20
Christmas, Nutcrackers, strip of 4, ATM bklt	$5	---
42c Any single: Drummer, Santa, King, Soldier	$1	$.20
42c Christmas, Madonna & Child	$1	$.20
42c Hanukkah	$1	$.20
42c Kwanzaa	$1	$.20
2009		
42c Alaska Statehood	$.85	$.20
42c Chinese New Year, Year of the Ox	$.85	$.20
42c Oregon Statehood	$.85	$.20
42c Edgar Allan Poe	$.85	$.20
$4.95 Redwood Forest, Priority Mail	$10	$8
$17.50 Old Faithful, Express Mail	$30	$15

2009	Unused	Used
42c Abraham Lincoln, four stamps	$3.40	---
Any single: Rail-splitter, Lawyer, Politician, President	$.85	$.20
42c Civil Rights Pioneers, Pane of 6	$5.25	---
Any single	$.85	$.20
10c Patriotic Banner	$.20	$.20
61c Richard Wright	$1.25	$.50
28c Polar Bear	$.60	$.20
28c Polar Bear, Coil	$.60	$.20
64c Dolphin	$1.25	$.50
44c Purple Heart	$.90	$.20
44c USA Flag	$.90	$.20
44c USA Flag, microprint USPS on right	$.90	$.30
44c USA Flag, microprint USPS in center	$.90	$.30
44c USA Flag, die cut 8.5	$.90	$.30
44c USA Flag, die cut 11	$.90	$.30
44c USA Flag from booklet	$.90	$.30
44c Wedding Ring	$.90	$.20
61c Wedding Cake	$1.20	$.50
44c The Simpsons strip of five	$4.50	---

2009	Unused	Used
Any single, Homer, Marge, Bart, Lisa, Maggie	$.90	$.20
44c Love, King of Hearts	$.90	$.25
44c Love, Queen of Hearts	$.90	$.25
44c Bob Hope, pane of 20	$17.50	---
Any single	$.90	$.20
44c Celebrate!	$.90	$.25
44c Anna Julia Cooper	$.90	$.20
44c Gulf Coast Lighthouses, five stamps	$4.50	--
Any single: Matagorda Island, Texas; Sabine Pass, La.; Biloxi, Miss.; Sand Island, Ala.; Fort Jefferson, Fla.	$.90	$.30
44c Early TV Memories, pane of 20	$18	---
Any single	$.90	$.20
44c Hawaii Statehood	$.90	$.20
44c Eid	$.90	$.20
44c Thanksgiving Day Parade, strip of 5	$4.50	---
Any single: Crowd, Drum Major, Musicians, Turkey Balloon	$.90	$.25
44c Gary Cooper, Legends of Hollywood pane of 20	$18	---
Any single	$.90	$.20
44c Supreme Court Justices, 4 stamps	$3.50	---
Any single	$.90	$.20

2009	Unused	Used
44c Kelp Forest Nature of America pane of 10	$9	---
Any single	$.90	$.20
44c Christmas Madonna & Child	$.90	$.20
44c Christmas secular block of 4	$3.50	---
Any single: Reindeer, Snowman, Gingerbread		
Man, Nutcracker	$.90	$.20
44c Christmas secular ATM block of 4		
(without upper design)	$3.50	---
Any single (same subjects)	$.90	$.30
44c Hanukkah Menorah	$.90	$.30
44c Kwanzaa Family	$.90	$.30
2010		
44c Chinese New Year, Year of the Tiger	$.90	$.20
44c Olympics Winter Games	$.90	$.20
$4.90 Mackinac Bridge, Priority Mail	$10	$4.50
$18.30 Bixby Creek Bridge, Express Mail	$36	$10
(44c) Liberty Bell (Forever)	$.90	$.20
44c Distinguished Sailors block of 4	$3.50	---
Any single: William S. Sims, Arleigh Burke, John McCoy, Doris Miller	$.90	$.25

2010	Unused	Used
44c Abstract Expressionists pane of 10	$9	---
Any single: Hans Hofmann, Willem de Kooning, Mark Rothko, Jackson Pollock, Arshile Gorky, Clyfford Still, Robert Motherwell, Joan Mitchell, Adolph Gottlieb, Barnett Newman	$.90	$.30
44c Bill Mauldin	$.90	$.20
44c Flags of Our Nation coil strip of 10	$9	---
Any single: US Flag and Mountain, Montana, Nebraska, Nevada, New Hampshire, New Jersey, New Mexico, New York, North Carolina, North Dakota.	$.90	$.20
44c Cowboys of the Silver Screen, block of 4	$3.75	---
Any single: Roy Rogers, Tom Mix, William S. Hart, Gene Autry.	$.90	$.20
44c Love, Pansies in a Basket	$.90	$.20
44c Adopt a Shelter Pet (in pane of 20)	$18	---
Any single: Wire-haired Jack Russell terrier, Maltese cat, Calico cat, Yellow Labrador retriever, Golden retriever, gray-white-tan cat, black-white-tan cat, Australian Shepherd, Boston terrier, orange tabby cat	$.90	$.20
44c Katharine Hepburn, Legends of Hollywood pane of 20	$18	---
Single stamp	$.90	$.20
64c Monarch Butterfly	$1.25	$.50

2010	Unused	Used
44c Kate Smith	$.90	$.20
44c Oscar Micheaux	$.90	$.20
44c Negro Leagues Baseball pair	$1.75	--
Either single, Players in game, Rube Foster	$.90	$.20
44c Sunday Funnies, strip of 5	$4.50	---
Any single: Beetle Bailey, Calvin and Hobbes, Archie, Garfield, Dennis the Menace	$.90	$.20
44c Scouting	$.90	$.20
44c Winslow Homer	$.90	$.20
44c Hawaiian Rain Forest, Nature of America pane of 10	$9	---
Any single	$.90	$.20
44c Mother Teresa	$.90	$.20
44c Julia de Burgos	$.90	$.20
44c Christmas, Angel With Lute	$.90	$.20
(44c) Evergreens (Forever), block of 4 in booklet	$3.75	---
Any single from booklet pane: ponderosa pine, Eastern red cedar, blue spruce, balsam fir	$.90	$.20
(44c) Evergreens (Forever), block of 4 in ATM pane	$3.75	---
Any single, same designs	$.90	$.20

42c Bette Davis

MAILING FOR CHARITY

In 1998, the USPS inaugurated a semi-postal stamp program, which has been a staple of some countries'government support of popular causes over the last 100 years. In practice, semi-postals are sold at a premium, with the amount in excess of the postal rate earmarked for a charity.

The first, for Breast Cancer Awareness, has raised more than $71 million over the years as its sale price has risen with rate increases. The Heroes of 2001 stamp (2002-04) raised $10.6 million for families of rescue workers killed during the attacks on the World Trade Center in New York City. The Stop Family Violence stamp (2003-2006) raised more than $3 million.

Semi-Postal Charity Stamps	Unused	Used
1998 32c + 8c Breast Cancer	$1.50	$.20
2002 37c + 11c Heroes of 2001	$1.75	$.40
2003 37c + 8c Stop Family Violence	$1.50	$.40

AIRMAIL 1918-2009

AMAZING COINCIDENCES

When people find out you collect stamps, some will ask you, "Do you have any upside-down airplanes?"

That stamp, the blue-and-red, 24-cent "Inverted Jenny" is the most famous postal error in the world, and only 100 copies existed when it was found. Incredibly, when the stamp collector who discovered the rarity left his home in Washington, D.C., the morning of May 14, 1918, to buy some new airmail stamps on the way to work, he told his wife he thought there might be a mistake to be found.

The first sheet of stamps he bought at the post office was fine, but he returned at noon, with another $30 he had withdrawn from his bank, and this time the postal clerk handed him the sheet of 100 inverted stamps.

Interestingly, when the inaugural flight of the new airmail service took off the next day from Washington on a flight to Philadelphia, the mail with the new stamps was in a plane (a model nicknamed "Jenny") with the same numbers on the fuselage (38262) as those on the stamp. That first flight ended 20 miles from Washington when the plane flipped over while landing in a soft field. It had become a real-life upside-down Jenny.

1918	Unused	Used
6c Curtiss Jenny, orange	$85	$45
16c Curtiss Jenny, green	$140	$50
24c Curtiss Jenny, carmine and blue	$150	$65
inverted	$175,000	---

1923		
8c Airplane Radiator & Propeller, dark green	$55	$20
16c Air Service Insignia, dark blue	$135	$40
24c DeHavilland Biplane, carmine	$200	$35

1926-27		
10c Biplanes & U.S. Map, dark blue	$5	$.75
15c Planes & Map, olive-brown	$6	$3
20c Planes & Map, yellow-green	$18	$3
10c "Spirit of St. Louis," dark blue	$13	$3.50

1928		
5c Beacon, carmine and blue	$8.50	$.80

1930		
5c Winged Globe, violet, perforation 11	$20	$.80

1930	Unused	Used
65c Zeppelin Over Atlantic, green	$335	$300
$1.30 Zeppelin Between Continents, brown	$600	$550
$2.60 Zeppelin & Globe, blue	$950	$900

1931-32		
5c Winged Globe, violet, perforation 10-1/2 x 11	$14	$.80
8c Winged Globe, olive-bistre, perforation 10-1/2 x 11	$5	$.40

1933		
50c Zeppelin, green	$155	$125

1934		
30c Winged Globe, dull orange	$5	$.20

1935-37 Transpacific Issues		
25c Pan Am Clipper, with date, blue	$2.50	$1.90
20c Pan Am Clipper, green	$20	$2.50
50c Pan Am Clipper, carmine	$20	$8.50

1938		
6c Eagle & Shield, dark blue and carmine	$1	$.30

1939	Unused	Used
30c Winged Globe, dull blue	$21	$2.25

1941-44 Transport Issue		
6c Cargo Plane, carmine	$.45	$.20
8c Cargo Plane, olive-green	$.50	$.20
10c Cargo Plane, violet	$3	$.20
15c Cargo Plane, brown-carmine	$5	$.40
20c Cargo Plane, bright green	$4.50	$.40
30c Cargo Plane, blue	$5	$.40
50c Cargo Plane, orange	$25	$5

1946-47		
5c DC-4 Skymaster, large, carmine	$.40	$.20
5c DC-4 Skymaster, small, carmine	$.40	$.20
10c Pan American Union Building, black	$.65	$.20
15c Statue of Liberty/New York City, blue green	$.60	$.25
25c Oakland Bay Bridge, blue	$2.25	$.20

1948		
5c Small Skymaster coil, carmine	$1.95	$1.70
5c New York City Map & Band, carmine	$.40	$.20

1949	Unused	Used
6c Small Skymaster, carmine	$.40	$.20
6c Alexandria, Va., Bicentennial, carmine	$.45	$.20
6c Small Skymaster, coil, carmine	$5.25	$.20

Universal Postal Union Issue		
10c Post Office Department Building, violet	$.40	$.30
15c Globe & Doves, ultraviolet	$.50	$.40
25c Stratocruiser & Globe, rose-carmine	$.75	$.60
6c Wright Brothers, magenta	$.55	$.25

1952		
80c Diamondhead, red-violet	$12	$2

1953		
6c Powered Flight, 50 years, carmine	$.40	$.25

1954		
4c Eagle in Flight, bright blue	$.40	$.20

1957		
6c Air Force, 50 years, blue	$.40	$.20

1958	Unused	Used
5c Eagle in Flight, red	$.40	$.25
7c Silhouette of Jet Airliner, blue	$.45	$.20
7c Silhouette of Jet, coil, blue	$4.50	$.20

1959		
7c Alaska Statehood, dark blue	$.50	$.20
7c Balloon Jupiter, blue and red	$.50	$.20
7c Hawaii Statehood, rose-red	$.50	$.20
10c Pan American Games, violet-blue and red	$.75	$.65

1959-67		
10c Liberty Bell, black and green	$2.50	$1
15c Statue of Liberty, full border, black and orange	$1	$.20
25c Abraham Lincoln, black and maroon	$1.20	$.20
13c Liberty Bell, black and red	$.90	$.20
15c Statue of Liberty, split border, black and orange	$.80	$.20

1960		
7c Silhouette of Jet, carmine	$.50	$.20
7c Silhouette of Jet, coil, carmine	$9	$.40

1962	Unused	Used
8c Jetliner & Capitol, carmine	$.45	$.20
8c Jetliner & Capitol, coil, carmine	$.50	$.20

1963		
15c Montgomery Blair, multicolored	$1.75	$1.20
6c Eagle on Rock, red	$.45	$.20
8c Amelia Earhart, multicolored	$.50	$.20

1964		
8c Robert H. Goddard, multicolored	$1	$.25
8c Alaska Purchase, brown	$.50	$.20
20c Columbia Jays, multicolored	$2	$.20

1968		
10c Runway of Stars, carmine	$.60	$.20
10c Runway of Stars, coil, carmine	$.90	$.20
10c 50 Years of Airmail, multicolored	$.90	$.25
20c USA & Jet, multicolored	$1.50	$.20

1969		
10c Moon Landing, multicolored	$.60	$.40

1971-73	Unused	Used
9c Delta Wing, red	$.45	$.40
11c Jetliner Silhouette, carmine	$.50	$.20
13c Winged Letter	$.50	$.20
17c Statue of Liberty, multicolored	$.90	$.20

1971-73		
21c USA & Jet, multicolored	$.80	$.20
11c Jetliner, coil, carmine	$.70	$.20
13c Winged Letter, coil, carmine	$.70	$.20

1972		
11c City of Refuge, Hawaii, multicolored	$.50	$.20
11c Winter Olympics Skiers, multicolored	$.70	$.45

1973		
11c Progress in Electronics, multicolored	$.50	$.25

1974		
18c Statue of Liberty	$.80	$.70
26c Mt. Rushmore	$1	$.20

1976	Unused	Used
25c Jetliner & Globes	$.75	$.25
31c Jetliner with Stripes	$1.25	$.30

1979		
31c Wright Brothers (large portraits)	$1.75	$.80
31c Wright Brothers (small portraits)	$1.75	$.80
21c Octave Chanute (large portrait)	$2.50	$2.40
21c Octave Chanute (small portrait)	$2.50	$2.40

1979		
25c Wiley Post (large portrait)	$2.75	$2.65
25c Wiley Post (small portrait)	$2.75	$2.65
31c Olympics High Jumper	$1.25	$1

1980-82		
40c Philip Mazzei, perforation 11	$1.75	$.30
40c Philip Mazzei, perforation 10-1/2 x 11-1/4	$5.50	$2
28c Blanche Stuart	$1.20	$.30
35c Glenn Curtiss	$1.40	$.40

1983	Unused	Used
Summer Olympics, block of 4	$9	---
Any single: Gymnastics, Hurdles, Basketball, Soccer	$2.25	$1
Summer Olympics, block of 4	$9	---
Any single: Shot Put, Rings, Swimming, Weight Lifting	$2.25	$1
Summer Olympics, block of 4	$10	---
Any single: Fencing, Cycling, Volleyball, Pole Vaulting	$2.50	$2
1985		
33c Alfred Verville	$1.40	$.60
39c Lawrence & Elmer Sperry	$1.75	$.60
44c Transpacific Airmail	$2.50	$.50
1985		
44c Junipero Serra	$2.35	$.90
1988		
44c Settling of New Sweden	$2.25	$2
45c Samuel Langley	$1.95	$.50
36c Igor Sikorsky	$1.75	$.70

1989	Unused	Used
45c French Revolution Bicentennial	$1.90	$1.90
45c Pre-Columbian Carved Figure	$2.25	$2

1989 Universal Postal Union Congress Issue		
Future Mail Delivery Methods, block of 4	$8.50	---
45c Any single: Space Shuttle, Hovercraft, Moon Rover, Shuttle Docking	$2	$1
U.P.U., souvenir sheet of 4	$8.50	---
45c Any imperforate single, as above	$2	$1

1990		
45c Tropical Beach	$1.90	$.90

1991		
50c Harriet Quinby	$2	$.40

1991		
40c William Piper (head clear of frame)	$1.60	$.50
50c Antarctic Treaty	$2.50	$.60
50c First Americans at Bering Land Bridge	$2.50	$1.50

1993	Unused	Used
40c William Piper (head touches upper frame)	$2.50	$.60

1999		
48c Niagara Falls	$2.25	$.80
40c Rio Grande	$1.60	$.60

2000		
60c Grand Canyon	$2.40	$.30

2001		
70c Nine-Mile Prairie, Nebraska	$2.75	$.75
80c Mt. McKinley	$3.25	$.60
60c Acadia National park	$2.40	$.50

2006		
63c Bryce Canyon	$2.50	$1
75c Great Smoky Mountains	$3	$1.25
84c Yosemite	$3	$1.25

2007	Unused	Used
69c Okefenokee Swamp	$1.40	$1.20
90c Hagatna Bay, Guam	$1.80	$1.60
2008		
72c 13-Mile Woods	$1.40	$1.20
94c St. John, Virgin Islands	$2	$1.75
2009		
79c Zion	$1.50	$1.25
98c Grand Teton	$1.90	$1.50

65c Zeppelin Over Atlantic, green

*$1.30 Zeppelin Between
Continents, brown*

$2.60 Zeppelin & Globe, blue

THE CHRISTMAS STAMP STORY

United States Christmas stamps may be the perfect collectible. For many individuals, the stamps' iconic images are comforting and significant. Since they have evolved to annual issues representing the religious and secular aspects of the holiday, collectors can find fine-art depictions of Biblical significance – the Nativity, angels and the

4c first Christmas stamp

Madonna and Child. Likewise, depictions of Santas, toys and decorations, for examples, are attractive to others.

At the same time, the stamps, to a remarkable extent, trace the technological innovations in U.S. stamp production in the last half-century.

Post Office Department officials were attracted and yet daunted by the prospect of issuing stamps specifically for use at the most popular mailing time of the year, when millions of greeting cards fly across the country. The disbursement of many millions of stamps to thousands of post offices and the subsequent retrieval of the unsold remainders after the season was challenging. And they

5c second Christmas stamp

5c third Christmas stamp, first U.S. se-tenant

understood the potential backlash that would follow the release of a stamp to support an essentially Christian holiday celebration.

The first Christmas stamp, issued in 1962, featured a wreath and candles in seasonal red and green, and bore the label "Christmas." It was an overwhelming hit with the general public. Nearly 862,000,000 stamps were printed,

*5c fourth
Christmas stamp,
Angel Gabriel*

almost seven times the normal commemorative production.

The next Christmas stamp, in 1963, had a printing of more than 1 billion copies. It depicted the huge national Christmas tree at the White House – and the label "Christmas."

It was among the first U.S. stamps to bear luminescent tagging, which allows high-speed, automated machinery to detect, position and cancel stamps on envelopes.

The 1964 Christmas issue featured the first four se-tenant stamps in U.S. history. The French term "se-ten-

5c fifth Christmas stamp, first Madonna & Child

ant" is used to describe stamps with different designs but attached. In years to come, se-tenant issues would become commonplace and include entire panes with 50 different stamps.

In 1965, the POD succumbed to a nationwide campaign in favor of a stamp that would show the religious basis for the season. An Angel Gabriel weather vane, it could be said, announced the next year's subject, a classic "Madonna and Child" artwork from the National Gallery of Art in Washington, D.C.

The same design was used in 1967 but in a larger

vertical format.

A second Angel Gabriel design, for the 1968 stamp, featured printing panes with multiple plate numbers corresponding to the colors used on a new press at the Bureau of Engraving and Printing. For collectors of plate blocks, the new format meant they had to save blocks of 20 stamps instead of four stamps with a single plate number.

5c sixth Christmas stamp, larger version of 1966

The Christmas Stamp Story

In an attempt to reduce handling costs during the busy end-of-the-year holiday season, the Postal Service experimented with pre-cancels, cancellation marks imprinted in four cities on some of the 1969 Christmas stamps. The design of the stamp was taken from a painting, Winter Sunday in Norway, Maine, by an unknown American artist.

6c seventh Christmas stamp, The Annunciation

6c eighth Christmas stamp, experimental precancel

6c ninth Christmas stamp, first Nativity

The Christmas Stamp Story

The precancel experiment, designed to reduce handling requirements, continued in1970, when two styles of Christmas stamps were issued for the first time. A religious-themed stamp showed a painting of the Nativity; and a secular-themed set of four had antique toys. During the production process, some of each were printed with precancels.

The two-tier Christmas package has continued. Interestingly, the first appearance of Santa Claus on a U.S. stamp came in 1972, 10 years into the program.

In 1974 the U.S. Postal Service offered another innovation – the first U.S. self-adhesive stamp, which was designed to self-destruct. Its illustration was derived from a dove-shaped weather vane atop George Washington's home at Mount Vernon, Va., and included the inscriptions, "Peace on Earth" and "Precanceled." Two crossed incisions were made on the stamp to guard against re-use.

The stamp was a disaster for the collecting community. When collectors tried to soak the stamps off the envelopes, they were often left with thin shreds. In addition, even on unused stamps, chemicals in the adhesive tended to migrate through the paper and leave blotchy stains on the face.

In 1975, a postal rate increase was expected, but its amount and its timing had not been decided, and the time-consuming printing and distribution of the Christmas stamps couldn't wait. The solution was to print the first U.S. stamps without a denomination as part of the design. Their rate would be whatever the Postal Rate Commission

6c ninth Christmas stamp, precancel

6c Christmas toys stamp, precancel

said it would be at the time of issue. It was left at 10 cents. The first-class mail rate went to 13 cents on Dec. 31.

The situation repeated itself for the 1991 Christmas stamps, which had a value of 29 cents.

There are many side stories that lend interest to a collection of Christmas stamps.

A 1984 Christmas stamp design was a crude, crayon drawing of Santa Claus by a third-grade student who won a nationwide contest in schools to design a stamp.

Two attempts by the Postal Service to salute the most

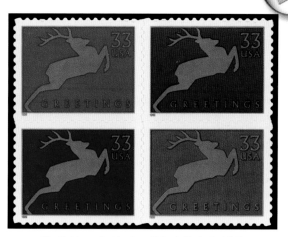

33c Christmas, Leaping Deer (intended to be Rudolph)

popular Christmas songs of the 20th century on stamps ended in abject failure. In the case of "White Christmas," postal officials were hemmed in by their own rules. In the case of "Rudolph the Red-Nosed Reindeer," design issues were the problem.

The 1988 Christmas stamp turned out to be a "stealth commemorative" to honor legendary songwriter Irving Berlin, whose 100th birthday occurred in 1988. It was against Postal Service practice to feature a living American on a stamp, but the postmaster general did his best to circumvent those rules. The secular stamp design that year showed a sleigh and a snowy village scene, which he hoped the public could dream of as a "White Christmas," one of Berlin's signature songs (he also wrote "God Bless America"). The stamp was dedicated in Berlin, N.H., and although he was invited to attend, the reclusive composer wasn't there.

Eleven years later, the Postal Service wanted to celebrate the 50th anniversary of the song about the reindeer Rudolph. Unfortunately, the copyright holders and the postal officials couldn't agree on a design, and at the last minute the USPS desperately pulled out a generic leaping deer based on an old illustration. The deer didn't have a red nose, but the stamp was dedicated at Rudolph, Wis.

However, the deer did have a long life. The next year, 2000, postal officials decided not to issue any new Christmas stamps, for the first time since 1962.

For most of those years – in fact, for 22 years straight – the U.S. religious Christmas stamp was a depiction of a classic Madonna and Child. That string was almost broken in 1995, when the Postal Service wanted to feature

Victorian images, including a fetching "Midnight Angel." When President Clinton heard of the plan to ignore the Madonna and Child, he objected, and postal officials hastened to rush a stamp with that image into production, along with the angel. Although there ended up being seven different stamp designs in a number of formats that year, not one of the stamps bore the label "Christmas." That was the first time since 1964 that the label was not included.

In 2005, when the USPS laid out a tray of Christmas cookies on its stamps, the only nod to the religious aspect of the season was a frosted angel cookie.

Beginning in 1996, the USPS also has issued non-Christian holiday stamps. The first was a stamp for the Jewish Hanukkah. A Kwanzaa stamp, for the secular Christmas-time holiday, followed in 1997, and an Eid Mubarek stamp for the Muslim holiday appeared in 2001. Each of those have been updated with new values or designs in subsequent years.

ERRORS, FREAKS AND ODDITIES

TREASURED MISTAKES

In no field besides the hobby of stamp collecting, perhaps, are the worst mistakes treasured so highly.

It is, in a sense, a tribute to the scrupulously meticulous art of design and production of many millions of stamps each year in the United States alone; so few mistakes emerge that they are considered rare and valuable. Indeed, the most famous and most expensive stamps in philately are errors – the "Inverted Jenny" airmail stamp of 1918, for example. (Its story is told in the introduction to the Airmail section of this book.)

"Inverts" (the shorthand term for stamps with a portion of their design upside-down in relation to another) comprise only one kind of error. There are many others, among them:

--Stamps printed in an unintended color or with one or more of their colors missing, under-inked or over-inked stamps, or multicolor stamps printed out of register.

*1c Fast Lake
Navigation,
green and black*

1c Fast Lake Navigation inverted error

--Stamps missing intended perforations or having too many sets of perforations or shifted perforations.

--Miscut stamps.

--Stamps with plate flaws, double impressions of some parts of the design or impressions on front and back.

--Design errors.

--Stamps printed on the wrong paper or printed so that the watermark is inverted.

All invite the exclamation, "Well, look at that!" when viewed, but their sheer numbers and varieties make it impossible to present in this field guide more than an

2c Red Cross with missing Greenland design error

*2c John Adams,
normal ink*

*2c John Adams
overinking freak*

*2c John Adams
underinking freak*

3c Pony Express design error

enticing introduction to this fascinating aspect of stamp collecting.

In a hobby whose participants have a propensity to categorize, they are known as errors, freaks, and oddities or "EFOs." With few exceptions, such as inverts, true errors must be totally missing an element. Also, according to custom, to be designated a true philatelic error, a stamp must not only represent a departure from printing perfection but also must have been sold to the public by the post office.

5c Washington, carmine, color error with two normal 2c stamps

6c Hemisfair '68, color shift error, left stamp normal, right error

Anomalies in any printing process are commonplace, especially when presses are starting up or shutting down. By one count, 16 different printers have produced error stamps. Generally, however, quality-control practices are so stringent that few are passed over and released for sale. Typically, commercial printers bundle up their paper waste and recycle it. In "security printing" -- of currency and stamps, for example – the waste is strictly accounted for during its destruction. Still, occasionally a dishonest worker will tuck some away and smuggle it out

6c Apollo 8, normal   *6c Apollo 8, perforation shift*

6c green color-missing error

of the plant.

Those pieces are known scornfully as "printers waste." They may be visually appealing –and, after all, their surprising appearance is what makes them desirable -- but they are illicit.

The first United States inverts appeared the first time the Post Office Department produced bi-colored stamps, in 1869. The next ones were in three values of the Pan-American Exposition commemoratives of 1901. The "Inverted Jenny" of 1918 was next, and 44 years later the government printed deliberate errors.

The sharp-eyed stamp collector who noticed the

10c Andrew Jackson, normal (1965-81 series)

10c Jackson misperforation error (changes design—denomination on right and no denomination)

upside-down background yellow on a pane of 4-cent Dag Hammarskjold stamps he bought at the post office in 1962 erred himself when he bragged publicly that his find would be worth a fortune. In response, the Post Office produced and released a huge number of the improperly printed stamps, effectively rendering the original error worthless.

A court of law subsequently found the government acted improperly in the case, but the collector earned only satisfaction and lasting fame, far from the jackpot he had anticipated.

In special souvenir sheets released in 2001, the

10c D.W. Griffith, color shift

Postal Service reproduced the inverts of 1901. They are distinguished by a year date in the lower-left margin of each stamp.

Hundreds of stamps exist with their colors omitted. The first was a Red Cross stamp issued in 1931. In that case, an errant piece of paper (possibly a fold) apparently blocked the application of the red color on one of the 99 million stamps printed.

Today's multi-color stamps offer a higher likelihood that one of the inks may be skipped, and the complexity of a design may hide the detection of a color-missing error. The snowy scene of the Christmas stamp of 1969 is one example. In the error (omitted light-green ink), the line of trees on the horizon appears light orange instead of green.

Other color-missing errors are more obvious. On the

15c Eagle perforation shift

15c Owls, color shift

*15c
Benjamin
Banneker,
imperforate
error
(printer's
waste)*

25-cent Lighthouse booklet stamps of 1990, for example, the white denominations are missing. On the 50-cent Jacqueline Cochran stamps of 1996, the aviatrix's name is omitted.

Color shifts on stamps can be more spectacular, but their value is generally much less. On the Hemisfair '68 stamp, for example, the shifted white locator moved the exposition from San Antonio, Texas, to somewhere in Florida. The Owl stamps of 1978 show a dramatic color shift.

Perforation mistakes may be discovered when a non-collecting member of the public tries to separate stamps for use and discovers he needs a scissors or finds perforations wandering. Early U.S. stamps were produced without means of separation, of course, and some since then have been produced imperforate deliberately.

"Imperforates," as they are known, must have intended perforations (or die cuts in today's self-adhesive stamps)

20c Metropolitan Opera, normal

20c Metropolitan Opera black color shift

25c Christmas stamp, missing curlicue on runner oddity (second stamp from bottom in left column)

25c Christmas stamp, gold
color missing error

29c Christmas stamp, normal

29c Christmas
stamp, double
perforation
shift error

25c Lighthouses booklet pane, normal

25c Lighthouses, white color missing error

missing. They fall into the "error" category. However, mis-perforated freaks can be the most dramatic. Sometimes an inadvertent paper fold will create "crazy perfs" wandering all over a pane of stamps. And in a few cases, such as the 10 cent Andrew Jackson stamp issued in 1967, misplaced perforations create a new stamp design – or a stamp with no denomination.

29c Flag Over Mt. Rushmore, normal

29c Flag Over Mt. Rushmore, dark brown

29c Flag and Mt. Rushmore, imperforate error

29c Flag and Mt. Rushmore, red color in middle "29" oddity

Most plate flaws are unobtrusive, and those collectors who like to seek them out with high-power magnifiers are known as "fly-speck philatelists." Other flaws are well known. For example, the "Broken Hat" variety on some copies of the 2-cent Columbian of 1893 features an easily discernible V-shaped gash in the hat of the knight standing to the left of Columbus and looking down (shown on page 49).

Design errors may take many forms. On the 1931 Red Cross stamp, for example, the artist did not include Greenland on the globe. The Pony Express commemorative stamp of 1940 depicts a horse in a pose that experts say would never occur.

The most notorious mistake in recent years, however, involved a miniature sheet picturing 16 "Legends of the

25c Honey Bee, imperforate error

25c Yosemite, imperforate error

West." The stamps had been printed and distributed by the Postal Service when descendants of one of the legends, rodeo bulldogger Bill Pickett, protested that the old photograph upon which his portrait was based was that of

23c USA reflecting flag, coils (three versions)

23c USA Presorted imperforate error

*29c Alaska
Highway,
normal*

*29c Alaska Highway
color shift (USA 29)*

Legends of the West, pane of 20

29c Bill Pickett

29c Bill Pickett design error

32c Flag Over Porch, normal

32c Flag Over Porch, color ink smear oddity

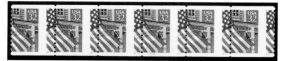

32c Flag Over Porch, perforation shift

another man, his brother. The USPS decided to recall the stamps and start over. Unfortunately, 183 of the panes of stamps already had been sold at four post offices ahead of the intended release date and had been used as postage.

Here was the quandary: The descendants of Pickett considered the design error to be an insult. The USPS wanted to save face and correct the mistake. Collectors and stamp dealers wanted access to the already-printed stamps, error and all. And the few people who owned the prematurely sold stamps had visions of getting rich.

The Postal Service's compromise solution was to sell, via a lottery system, 150,000 of the erroneous panes to the public at face value of $5.80 plus $2.90 priority rate shipping. At auction today, the error sheet sells typically at more than $250.

50c Jacqueline Cochran, black color missing error (name)

RESOURCES

STAMP COLLECTING ORGANIZATIONS:

American Philatelic Association
100 Match Factory Place
Bellefonte PA 16823
www.stamps.org

EFO Collectors Club
PO Box 1125
Falls Church VA 22041
www.efocc.org

American Topical Association
P.O. Box 8
Carterville IL 62918-0008
www.americantopicalassn.org

COMMERCIAL EXPERTIZERS

Commercial "expertizers" can judge whether a specific stamp is what you think it is. Here are three respected organizations:

American Philatelic Expertizing Service
The American Philatelic Center
100 Match Factory Place
Bellefonte PA 16823
www.stamps.org

Philatelic Foundation
70 W. 40th St.
15th Floor
New York NY 10018
www.philatelicfoundation.org

Professional Stamp Experts Inc.
PO Box 6170
Newport Beach CA 92658
www.psestamp.com

GENERAL-INTEREST PUBLICATIONS:

Linn's Stamp News
P.O. Box 29
Sidney OH 45365-0029
www.linns.com

Mekeels's & Stamps Magazine
42 Sentry Way
Merrimack NH 03054-4429

About the author

Maurice D. Wozniak has collected United States stamps for more than 50 years, starting as a child after he became interested in a small collection that his uncle had. After a 30-year career in journalism as a reporter and editor for large daily newspapers in the Midwest, he edited news periodicals for the stamp hobby, first as editor of the weekly Stamp Collector and biweekly The Stamp Wholesaler, and he finally became editor of a line of stamp catalogs before retirement.

Always fascinated by the stories inherent on postage stamps, he wants to encourage others to discover the enjoyment he has found.

Wozniak continues to write essays and free-lance magazine articles on stamp-collecting topics. He also remains active in the social underpinnings of the hobby. He has served several years as president of the Wisconsin Federation of Stamp Clubs and has helped organize its annual stamp shows. He is a member of the American Philatelic Society and other collector groups within the hobby.

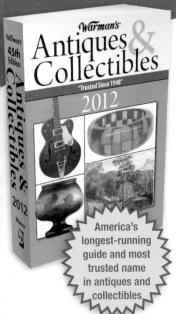